DESIGN WITH
PLANT MATERIAL

ABOUT THE AUTHOR

Marian Aaronson is an internationally known flower arranger, who has travelled extensively to teach, lecture, judge and demonstrate the art of flower arranging. Over the years she has developed an individual style which is progressive and inspiring to others. Her first book *The Art of Flower Arranging* is now in its Fourth Edition, and this volume of *Design with Plant Material* is a Second Edition.

MARIAN AARONSON

DESIGN
WITH
PLANT MATERIAL

GROWER BOOKS
LONDON

Grower Books
49 Doughty Street
London WC1N 2LP

© Marian Aaronson 1972
First published 1972
Second Edition 1979

ISBN 0 901361 12 7

Designed and produced in
Great Britain
by Sharp Print Management
Fakenham, Norfolk

Dedicated to my Mother and Father.

Thanks are due to Ken Lauder for his skilful photography; to my son Robin for his help; and to my family and flower arranging friends for their support and encouragement.

CONTENTS

INTRODUCTION

In my first book *The Art of Flower Arranging* I tried to show how rewarding it is for the arranger to progress from the basic to the more creative aspects of arranging; how design, once appreciated, is the key to self-expression and interpretation of ideas. In this book, I would like to take you a step further along the road of progress to even freer styles. I want you to realise that there is no limit to the possibilities of something new and fresh and challenging in designing, that it need never become boring or repetitive. No true artist is ever really satisfied or complacent about his or her achievements, but strives continually to improve the standard, and to add to the range of creative possibilities. This discontent is often the spur to progress, though the visible form one is able to give to every new idea does not always come easily. But then, rewarding, satisfying achievements seldom come without hard work and effort.

The character of flower arranging has changed considerably over the years. Changes have come with fresh discoveries, with the need to find newer and better techniques, new outlooks, new objectives, and the evolution of one style to another.

The arranger today is given greater opportunities to design imaginatively with tutors who encourage the student to be creative rather than imitative. This constructive approach involves the student more fully in the learning process — it encourages the arranger to experiment with the material, to be adventurous in using it and to discover fresh ways of designing rather than copy the set and stereotyped, which tends to produce arrangements all looking very similar and limited in style. Creative teaching fosters originality and natural flair.

Schedule makers are relaxing restrictions to allow the exhibitor more scope and liberty. Improved staging and a more imaginative approach to the presentation of exhibits encourages ingenuity and a more adventurous outlook. The class titles have become so much more challenging and inspiring, which demands more progressive and imaginative styles.

All the arts tend to be affected by the same general trends and current influences, so there is a similarity of outlook, concept and practices at any one time. The techniques, methods and media of one are often borrowed by another. This brings new dimensions or extensions to each art form. Today we see paintings of a three-dimensional nature, with objects standing out of the frame. There are coloured sculptures and sculptures made of metal, wire or plastic. New extensions of flower arranging are mobiles, stabiles, the collage, montage, assemblages or constructions, many of which hardly qualify as *flower* arrangements. It is clear that the boundaries of flower arranging, like those of the other arts, are becoming increasingly less sharply defined. New concepts, new theories, new images, have carried it to a wider, larger sphere, where flowers and their arranging are only a part. As in the other arts, a greater range of materials and ways of usage becomes valid for designing purposes.

Furthermore, greater knowledge, experience and understanding has developed a strong appreciation of design, which has raised flower arranging to a highly artistic level, from a mere decoration to a creative art form. In this larger realm the arranger evaluates the medium more for its designing possibilities than its horticultural perfection, for its abstract qualities rather than its mere surface prettiness. This leads to a new way of seeing and use. Material is utilised in whatever way or style suits the design purpose — non-realistically or in a distorted, changed, or completely altered form. New patterns, new shapes, new images, will therefore keep emerging, some acceptable, some causing controversy, but all adding interest, diversity, and the stimulation needed to keep the art alive and moving forward. Design itself has become the art, not just a means to an end.

As a result of all these developments, 'Flower Arranging' no longer seems a comprehensive enough description for the art in its present form, and in the wider context 'Design with Plant Material' is perhaps more appropriate.

Plant material as an art medium is unique. It consists of intricately constructed items with a life of their own — not inanimate like clay or paint or stone, but objects with their own individual identity. This can be difficult to ignore and to dissociate from what is familiar and real.

Its vitality and aliveness is part of its charm. Form, shape, colour, and texture are already established by nature. This gives the arranger a wide choice, variety, and inspiration. On the other hand these same assets make it a medium difficult to control fully, and manipulate for the desired result.

It is the bringing together of its infinitely varied, strange, and beautiful parts into a meaningful form that is the challenge and task of the designer.

COLOUR PLATES

COLOUR PLATE 1 (see page 21) — *There is tremendous textural interest in the skeletonised opuntia used here. Its delicate tracery seems an unbelievable transformation from the fleshy, prickly pads of the plant in its natural form. The many and diverse shapes combine to make an interesting pattern, with pleasing depth and movement. A silvery-grey piece of weathered wood completes the outline. The dried items accentuate the freshness and vibrancy of the living plants; each is enhanced through contrast. A framework of this soft, neutral hue complements and flatters most colour harmonies, and it is interesting to experiment with different combinations.*

COLOUR PLATE 2 (see page 32) — 'Blitz' — *An interpretative arrangement to depict the burning of the old church during the Blitz. The charred gorse has a dramatic, expressive line, and is arranged in two black, cylindrical containers whose texture is semi-gloss to offset that of the black wood. Black, always a wonderful foil for brilliant colours, lends added zest to the colour of the clivia flowers. Greenery would have detracted from the sharpness of the colour contrast, and reduced the effectiveness of the interpretation. The completed arrangement was placed on a low, semi-circular table with an orange top against the light wood of the altar-rails. It seemed an appropriate illustration of the past and preparation for depiction of the present.*

COLOUR PLATE 3 (see page 34) — *This is quite a large arrangement, made with bold, attractive items, that would add interest and a touch of excitement to the appropriate setting. A plain background would set off the beauty of line, space, and colour; one with an interesting texture would further the interest of the voids. The container is plain stoneware of a very simple but pleasing design, and matches the cane in texture and colour. Even without flowers, the design is pleasing because of the arresting movement made by the cane. The weight of the container reduces the risk of its toppling over — always a consideration in the home.*

COLOUR PLATE 4 (see page 38) — *One usually thinks of mass in terms of profusion, and 'line' as associated with sparsity and clarity. The modern mass arrangement, however, is often based on a definite line structure. This is likely to result in a more streamlined, uncluttered version of the mass, with the items organised to comply with the required shape. There is a more controlled rhythm, a more positive use of space than in the true mass, where colours, forms, and textures often merge and tend to lose their separate identity. The marble urn, of classical line, balances the material without giving the eye an impression of too much weight. Its colour is light and delicate.*

COLOUR PLATE 5 (see page 51) – *The ragged texture of the bark is used to interpret the destructive element in nature. Erosion or Corrosion is conveyed in the line and form of the design. The height proportions are purposely exaggerated, and the balance given a precarious quality. The line and form of the container repeating that of the plant material strengthens the theme.*

COLOUR PLATE 6 (see page
74) — *Present-day art is often
characterised by a feeling for
the actual materials used and a
pre-occupation with their
specific qualities — the
qualities, for example, of paint
as paint rather than as a vehicle
for the representation of
something else. In Flower
Arranging, we find the
corresponding trend in designs
with full emphasis on textures
and full use of objets trouvées,
where the material takes on
added importance and there is
greater awareness of its
essential qualities. In a collage,
with the materials in close
juxtaposition, as they are here,
textures and forms are strongly
emphasised; we are strongly
aware of the roughness of the
skeletonised opuntia and the
variation of the surface
qualities of the silver birch
bark. The background,
roughened up with sand,
Polyfilla, and powder paint,
is adapted to the textures of
the plants so as to give further
emphasis.
(View horizontally)*

COLOUR PLATE 7 (see page 80) — *A construction made with fresh material that dries well; the reeds were still green when the picture was taken, but later they will change to a light brown. The stalks are glued to a thicker dried stalk; the separate pieces can then be angled for movement and depth. Constructions of this nature could well be developed into a new category of arrangement. In this case, flowers have been used, but there is also room for the flowerless variety exemplified on pages 81 to 88. Might we perhaps see 'A construction with natural plant material' as a class title in the future? It could lead to interesting and provocative innovations.*

COLOUR PLATE 8 (see page 90) — *As in the arrangement on page 91, this pattern also shows 'truth to material'. The structural characteristic of each item is exploited, so that we are made more aware of its special features and its abstract qualities; the strength of the sword-like leaves, the pattern of the variegated flax, the rhythmic quality of the dracaena, the delicacy in the structure of the reeds. All are combined to form a pattern of varying linear and spatial interest. This particular composition, seen as it is in colour, has the added interest of rhythm created by the shades, tints and tones of green.*

COLOUR PLATE 9 (see page 94) — *This is an impression of a mobile and a stabile visualised in picture form. It has a light-hearted, lyrical quality, and, without actually moving, gives an impression of animation. This is because of its line, especially that of the radiating pattern of the top grouping ('Star-dust'?). The colours of the tiny flowers and grasses add gaiety and sparkle. The 'moon' containers help to define the two planes and to increase the picturesque effect.*

COLOUR PLATE 10 –
Rotating rings of clear perspex form an ever-changing elliptical pattern of light that is wholly enchanting in this more elegant version of the mobile. The visual lightness and light-reflecting quality of the perspex makes it ideal for a construction of this nature. This is a case of the flower arranger borrowing from another medium. It is quite a logical progression in the search for more adventurous ways of developing ideas. At the same time the non-living element does harmonise with the jewel-like colours of the dyed plant material.

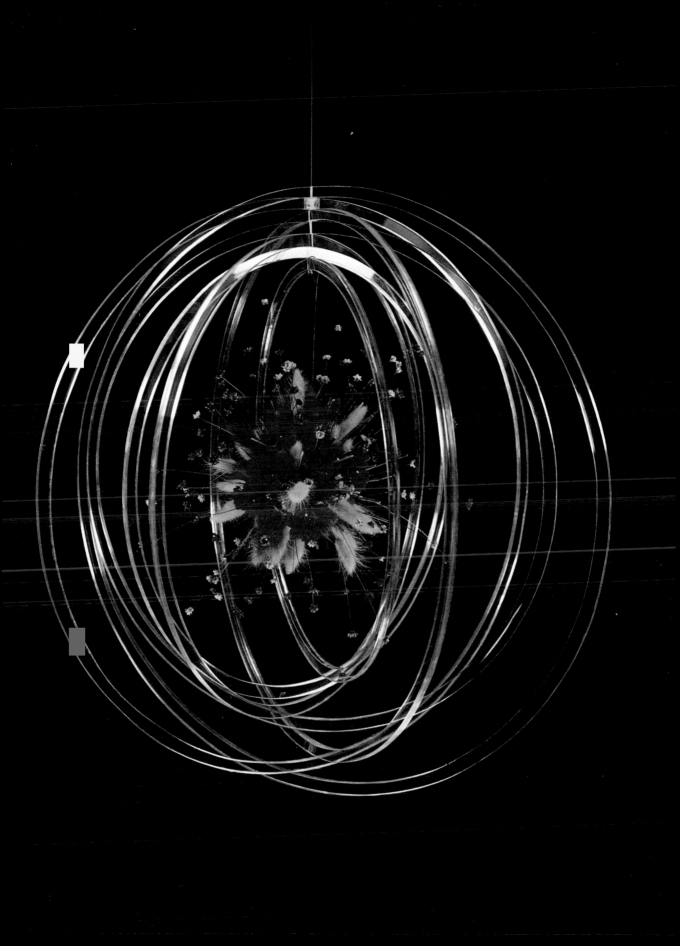

COLOUR PLATE 11 —
*This type of design extends
beyond the conventional
and is a 'construction' of
natural plant material.
It relies on form and
pattern, and light and shade
effects for visual appeal. The
hollow, woody stems of varying thickness were grouped,
and glued together to create
a free form sculpture.*

COLOUR PLATE 12 —
What drama of line, form and colour the Heliconia has! Here it is complemented by 2 curved stalks and strips of curled Eucalyptus bark, in a tall brown pottery container.

1

A NEW LOOK AT DESIGN

In the early stages of flower arranging the design principles are studied, the simple basic styles practised. Once mastered, the arranger should reach out for something more challenging and move to a more advanced level. The eye is now more trained to what is balanced, proportionate and harmonious in a design. Knowledge and experience should give the confidence to adapt the general to a more personal pattern, to be imaginative rather than repetitive.

One is guided by the same principles and the aim is still for an orderly, rhythmic pattern, but the designing procedure can be varied, and the principles modified con siderably to suit a particular style or situation. This gives greater flexibility and freedom to be creative.

With balance, for instance, one is taught at the beginning that the lightest item (in visual weight), the palest colour, the smallest form should be at the top of the design, the heaviest, darkest, and the largest form at the base. As one progresses it is possible to alter this for different styles, often to produce a more interesting balance. Sometimes perfect balance produces a static effect and experimenting with a line, form or colour out of balance can bring about a more lively and stimulating composition.

Very often, in an abstract arrangement, the most dramatic item is at the top of the design. This need not make the arrangement un-balanced, for other factors can compensate — an eye-catching area of space further down, perhaps, or an interesting line which carries the eye to other parts of the design. It is a more subtle balance, which must be carefully controlled to preserve the visual appeal of the arrangement. It is indeed an important factor in the freer style, and one that strongly affects its success.

Study examples of the more free-style type of arrangements, to see how balance has sometimes been achieved by the subtlest of means — by the pull of a leaf here countered by a slight change of direction there. With your own arrangements you will discover that often only the slightest adjustment is needed for a pleasing equilibrium.

Experiment with the material in different placements to see which combination gives the most interesting balance. Try putting the first placement deliberately out of balance, then adjust this with the next item. Repeat the process with the third and fourth placements. You will appreciate the rhythms and tensions created, how you are controlling these, and getting the right impact from the pattern created. This is a more interesting way of working than the old repetitive method and gives greater scope for variety.

You are now designing as you go along, rather than to a pre-planned formula; for each item really brings a different force to the design, and it is

FIG 1 — *Spaces and solids are so distributed as to give variety and an interesting balance to this design. The heaviness and solidity of the wood is balanced by the areas of empty space created by the ivy twigs, which are themselves sufficiently varied to prevent monotony. Note the attractive space on the left where the base of the wood unites with the twig. The movement created forces the eye upwards and outwards. The lower placements on the right hand side have the opposite effect. The process is repeated throughout the design to produce a pleasing rhythm and a forceful balance. Solids are also organised to give maximum movement combined with balance — notice the varying directional lines of the flowers, how this affects the rhythm too. Again, the leaves placed in different planes increase depth and benefit movement. The base here is added as much to repeat the rhythm of the design as for a pleasing impression of stability.*

better to experiment and to manoeuvre for the best result, rather than assume there is only one solution at the start. For example, the rhythm and force of the design is often improved with a little juggling of the areas of interest.

You will appreciate by now how one heavy, static area draws the eye continuously to it. The aim in modern designing is to space out the interest for a more continuous eye pause throughout and a more animated rhythm. Solid is balanced with space here and there to avoid monotony and repetition.

Proportions do not always have to be conventional either. It is possible to adjust these to suit the style or the interpretation. Exaggerated proportions are often used to emphasise line, for instance, where more than the customary height of plant material stresses the upward movement. Nothing should reduce this, like too much weight near the rim of the container, or underneath it. A base is not always necessary, unless it adds to or repeats the dominant line. Make everything in the design work for the required effect.

One uses the same initiative with all the other principles of design, adapting and modifying each one for the most stimulating and expressive composition. What you are really doing now is using the methods you have learnt to make your own personal design structure, developing as you go a distinctive and individual style of arranging.

FIG 2 – *The conventional transition is often omitted from an abstract design. This can give a more dramatic rhythm or a sharper silhouette. The two white hyacinths here represent a sudden jump in visual weight from the thin reed stalks. In spite of this disparity in scale, however, the overall proportions and balance of the design are maintained by the weight of the space areas and the two containers. In this style of arrangement sharp contrasts in scale or proportion are also often used to emphasise the qualities of the material.*

2

CHARACTERISTICS OF
THE MODERN DESIGN

(a) Restraint and Simplicity

Let us now consider certain features most characteristic of the modern design. The modern flower arrangement is a more compact, streamlined form. Shapeless, overfilled masses have given way to more sculptural compositions with cleaner, more definite lines. Space is appreciated and used more positively to give a more dynamic and lively pattern. Simplicity and clarity have greater impact than a confused layout, so the aim is for an uncluttered pattern which gives full value to the special features of the items used. Superfluous fillers reduce the force of the design; so essentials only are included whether a smaller or greater amount of material is used.

This simplifying process makes it easier to arrive at a conclusion, to get a theme or an idea across successfully. When too many different features are brought in there is a likelihood of the original objective being lost. It is often possible to get maximum interest with a minimum range; one dominant shape or line perhaps, but with changes of form or direction within the main pattern to avoid monotony.

In Fig. 3 opposite, a design featuring movement, the main motion is circular. The two containers, base, shape of flower, and twist of wisteria vine all accent this. The two vertical lines give variation without confliction. Since movement is the subject, the line is kept as clear and uncluttered as possible.

The more you look and study the restrained arrangement, the more obvious it is that relatively few elements are needed for effective interpretation. The few well chosen, well placed items are more likely to produce unity and completeness than an unrestrained collection. The controlled design is usually the most impressive. This does not always mean a severely sparse, stark design. Even when using a quantity of material there has to be a simplicity of purpose, a certain restraint to avoid the gross and the overstated. 'An avoidance of excess' is one of the dictionary definitions of restraint. Too many ideas, too many spectacular items, too much variety all weaken the design.

In assessing one's work the question very often should not be 'What else can I put in?' but 'What do I take out?' It is often astonishing what one leaf less does to the rhythm and force of the design; how the extra flower here and there can spoil the impact, or weaken the balance of a space area. A degree of severity in a design gives a sense of repose, like lack of clutter in dress, or a shop window. The beauty of simplicity draws attention and holds the eye much longer than the overdecorated. What really happens in the clear cut, sculptural composition is that in eliminating the non-essentials the arranger finally ends up with the simple basic design in all its dramatic simplicity. The basic form is often more compelling without the additional textures or colours brought in to highlight or to soften its severity because of the division of interests created.

Colour effects can also be overdone. An unrestrained use may spoil the colour harmony. Again, a few well chosen colours can have more impact than too many spectacular hues where one cancels out the effectiveness of the other. Colour can be controlled for maximum impact by playing up to the particular effect required, whether this is subtlety of hue or the drama of strong colour contrast. In either instance one should refrain from adding colour that detracts from the dominant scheme. A lot of green leaves would reduce the sharp colour contrast of, say, black and orange. It would not be *wrong,* but the pungency of the colour scheme would be lessened. In a quiet colour harmony of greys and browns, a touch of bright colour would again create a different effect. It would be interesting, but might reduce the quality of subtlety if that was the original intention.

When a spectacle of colour is planned, many colours can of course be used — several vibrant or clashing hues if necessary. But even here the amount and distribution must be controlled. There must be rhythm and sequence of colour effects for impact so that the dramatic colour spectacle is also harmoniously presented.

One uses the same principle

with all the other elements letting the dominance of one texture, line or shape work for the most direct, least complicated impression to give full value to the most important quality of the design.

The meticulous arrangement which looks so 'simple' calls for great control in the selection and distribution of the units for the perfect balance of shape with space, form with texture or colour with line. Errors stand out more sharply, and are not as easily camouflaged as in the profusion of the mass, but the attributes are that much more noticeable for the same reason.

FIG 4 – *The beautiful form of the two lilies is fully exploited in this arrangement by the stark simplicity of their setting. Filler material would have reduced design impact, and the value of space would have been lost. But when the flowers are framed in space as here, their qualities are greatly enhanced, and the texture and form of the wood receive much greater emphasis.*

FIG 5 — *The entire drama of the form and texture of the two lysitichum leaves is preserved in this simple presentation. They make an excellent foil for the flowers, contrasting with their colour and texture, and harmonising with their sculptural quality. The container seems to establish the atmosphere of strength and durability which also pervades the material.*

FIG 6 — *The restraint of this arrangement lends to its big, bold items the clarity needed for full emphasis of their impressive qualities. The handsome grey-green and charcoal container needs the complement of strong outline material. The two dried dark brown echium stalks provide a good continuation of line, and form a flattering framework for the one lily, which seems all the more serene and dignified in isolation. The two broad leaves are those of bergenea.*

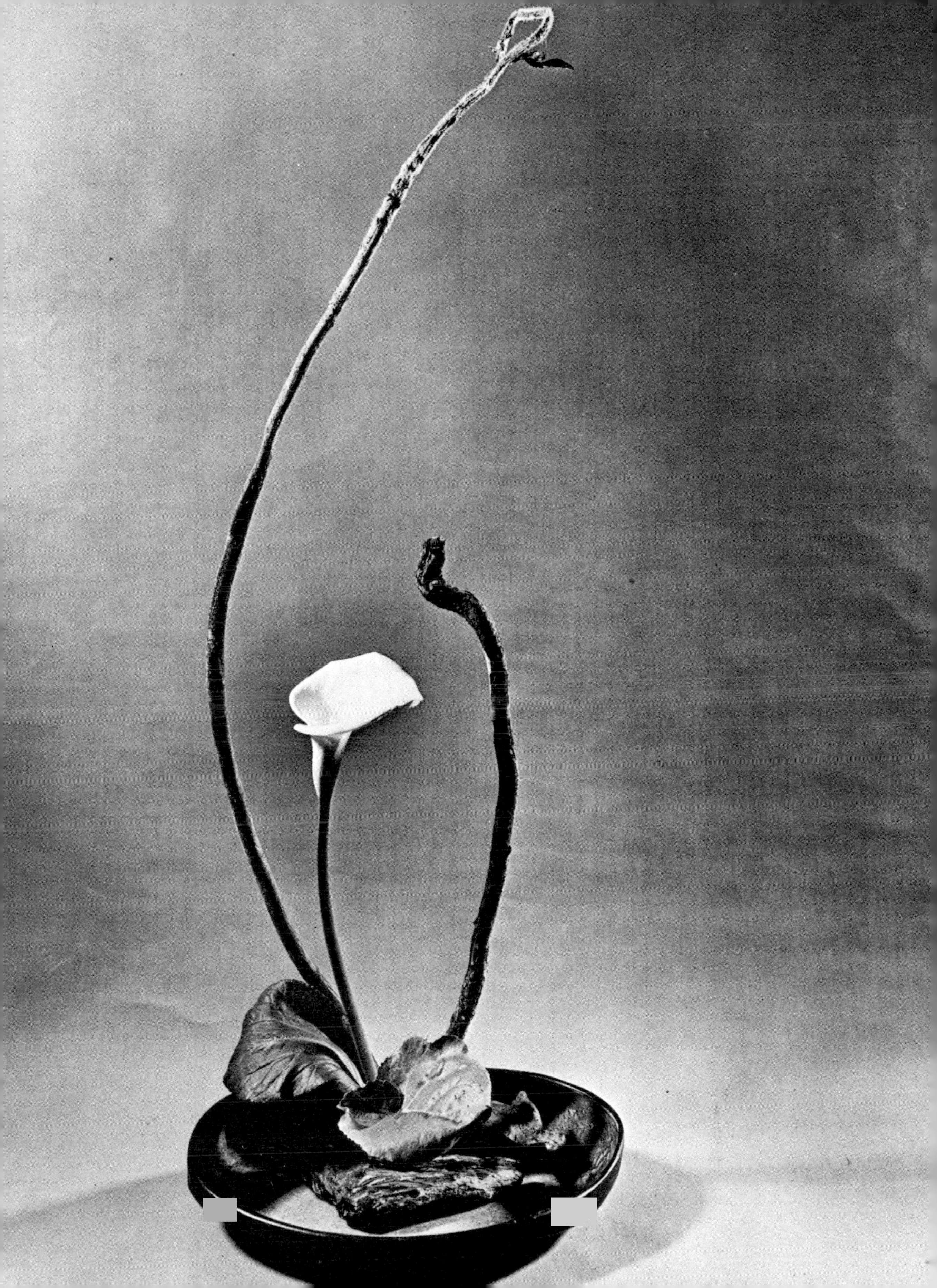

(b) Space and Movement

The arranger uses the elements of space and movement more dramatically in a sparse arrangement than in massed groupings. With careful placement of each item to create line and shape, space is moulded into the structure of the design to play as important a part as the solid items. Space now is not just an empty area, it is part of the strength and impact of the design. Just as superfluous material can reduce the design force, overcrowding the space areas weakens the vigour of the arrangement.

In the examples here, look at the proportion of the space areas to the plant material. Try and visualise extra flowers in Fig. 7. Another leaf in Fig. 8, filler material in Fig. 10. You can imagine what these additions would do to the spatial forces.

By training the eye to see and to understand the power of space, these forces can be controlled and used positively. It is not just keeping plant material to a minimum, it is placing this for the most rhythmic effect and greatest spatial interest. The eye responds to a pleasant fluid movement between one area and another. This is done by creating tensions, a pull-and-push effect which draws the eye inwards, then outwards; without these tensions the design lacks life.

I expect you have often looked at an arrangement, your own or someone else's, and wondered why it failed to move you in any way. This can be a perfectly balanced, efficiently constructed one with no *obvious* design fault, yet lacking in sparkle and that certain something the arrangement one immediately responds to seems to have. The trouble so often is this lack of vitality — there is no animation, no spark.

Art is illusion, and it takes its meaning for us through the imagination. By creating the illusion of space the imagination is stimulated, and we can experience the form of the arrangement in its deepest sense.

Optical illusion increases the sense of depth. The plant material in Fig. 7 is placed with the leaf moving diagonally to the right, the strelitzia flowers in an opposing plane. The two euphorbia stems also 'move' in separate directions with the line of the base continuing the rhythm. The movement and sense of depth created by these solid items is further enhanced by the illusionary depth of the enclosed area of space. The eye is drawn right through and beyond, into what looks deep and far away; this strengthens the imaginative quality of the design.

Again, in Fig. 8 the two lilies are placed to give the maximum sense of depth with only two flowers. One is directed upwards, the other forward, but the greatest illusion of depth is created by the spaces defined by the salix twigs. In this arrangement, depth is further accentuated by light and dark values, advancing and receding qualities. Notice how the dark leaves pull the eye in, how the white stones and the lower lily draw it out again. The rhythms created animate a design that could otherwise be rather flat.

You can see how dark and light areas improve depth and movement even more clearly in Fig. 9. The structure of the dried strelitzia leaves provide an exciting rhythm, carrying the eye in many directions and creating beautiful space areas. But the two light pink anthuriums add a terrific forwards and backwards pull through the contrast of light with dark. They also add a sharp difference of texture to further the activity of the design — the smooth, matt surfaces tend to recede, the shiny, glossy ones to advance. And so do the rough, pitted stones with a more noticeable texture. The rough and smooth surface variations in the base work in the same way. What a lot one can learn assessing the effects of various elements and how they can be controlled to achieve the desired result.

Crossing lines can make us more aware of space, and help to create depth. Without the diagonally directed teasle stalks in Fig. 10 the spatial force of the design would be considerably weaker. Imagine this arrangement with just straight lines. The eye would move in a vertical direction only, and be attracted to the line of the plants more than the space around them. As soon as the line is made more varied with the top teasle opposing the line of the next, the lower cutting across the two verticals, tensions are created that make the eye move up and down between the spaces now brought more to our notice. Space is being moulded and made active; the arrangement becomes a sculptural construction. The monstera leaf in Fig. 7 overlapping the plane of the other items gives an illusion of depth where actual, physical depth is comparatively little. The crossing lines of the two stems in the same arrangement break the vertical line suggested by the flowers, adding more energy and excitement to the rhythm.

Note that in all these examples there is space between the last placements and the base or container to offset their visual weight and to avoid a static, ground-anchored impression.

The weight of a space area varies with its nature. Often a small enclosed area has greater eye pull than a large open one. This affects the balance and visual appeal of the design. The small striking space area made by the curved strelitzia leaf in the bottom left-hand corner in Fig. 7 compensates the larger open area created by the longest leaf. Again, notice the strength of the triangular space in Fig. 10.

Clearly, space becomes the energy of the design. You will find it a great refreshment to use its forces in a variety of ways to give the essential life to your work.

FIG. 7 *(left) and* FIG. 8

FIG. 9 *(left) and* FIG. 10

3

A NEW LOOK AT PLANT MATERIAL

With greater control of the designing procedure, the arranger is able to be more adventurous also in the choice of material. A beginner usually feels committed to three types of plants — outline, focus, and filler type material. It is an easy way to work out proportion, balance and transition. After a while the keen arranger will vary the formula, and not be so rigid in the choice of items.

As she gets better acquainted with the medium, and with constant handling and experimenting, the arranger should discover even more effective usage; ever-varying combinations which show the materials in a different light, or display their special qualities more effectively. This is an absorbing search which can lead to exciting discoveries.

Very often a whole design can be made using only one type of material. This at first would seem a contradiction of the principles taught. How can one have variety, contrast, dominance and so on this way, you might ask? But by displaying the various aspects in an interesting, varied way, the arrangement can have all the attributes of a good design, and it does give emphasis to the special charm of the plant. Like the onion stalks in Fig. 11. Here there is variety of line and spaces in the structure of the plants, so the eye is not bored with monotonous movement. One can study all the detail, and see the strange formation of growth without the distraction of filler material. Leaves at the base would in fact have reduced the force of the design, and detracted from the spatial interest. Instead, the necessary accent is provided by the triangular pattern made with the stalks. These are fascinating plants to grow. The onions spring out at the end of the stalks in clusters. The botanical name is *Allium cepa proliferum.*

If you are not quite ready to eliminate as drastically as this, some very interesting arrangements can be made by combining materials at varying stages of growth. Plants are attractive at more than one phase; in bud, bloom and maturity. The poppy is a good example, especially the annual variety with its lovely seedheads. The stalks bend rather obligingly too, which gives a lot of depth and movement to a sparse design, as in Fig 12. I like the frilly, double variety with its jewel colours and the flowers contrast well in texture with the smooth seedheads to give the design plenty of interest.

When one is concentrating like this on the special characteristics of the media, it is easy to go a step further in the attempt to emphasise more fully a specific quality, or to use the plant in a new form. Some of the tree ivy we pick is long and straight and not very interesting, but stripped and bent into new patterns it becomes much more exciting. Straight spindly reeds are not very inspiring either, but are very effective bent into geometric patterns for abstract shapes. Broom can be coaxed and teased to give a lot of movement, and bleached white it has terrific impact. In this way one is often more aware of the nature and potential of a plant, so it is not really an insult to Nature as we often accentuate qualities that might otherwise be overlooked.

Some materials are actually improved with a little treatment. Wood, twigs and dried leaves that have lost their lustre or are perhaps not very spectacular in their natural state, can become quite dramatic painted black or gold. Wood is adaptable to a number of changes. It can be blackened, bleached or painted any colour; made rougher or smoother to increase its textural value. Also many natural items have an interesting texture that can be intensified, like bark or fungi. I once saw an enormous brown and cream fungus made glossy with varnish. It emphasised all the wonderful markings and gave a most exotic surface quality. The intriguing shape of the one featured in Fig. 13 lent to being used as a piece of natural sculpture. It may not coincide with the more popular idea of beauty, and you might not want it around the home. Nevertheless it makes an absorbing study in form and texture, and its strange formation stirs the imagination. It is weird, but also wonderful.

And so is the prickly pear *(opuntia)* in Colour Plate 1. In its skeletal state it is quite ethereal, and lends a very distinctive surface quality to an arrangement, as many skeletonised items do. Their transparency adds depth and distance, and a certain mystique, when colour and shape is viewed through their structure. The skeletonising process was done by Nature, not by me.

In an altered form the material often has this greater design force. It also increases its abstract quality which gives a less realistic effect. Pliable, easy to bend items are useful in abstract work to create new form structures. In this freer realm the arranger has greater scope to be inventive. She can experiment boldly with the material to present it differently, seeing it more as units of design rather than as horticultural specimens with specific and characteristic growth habits, suggesting certain usage.

This should become apparent as the different styles are discussed and illustrated. The material itself can prompt the nature of the design, for the message is there in the medium. Some plants call for the more conventional use and look best in naturalistic settings. The structure and character of certain flowers are not conducive to manipulation and these look unnatural and unhappy forced into stylised patterns. It really is better to let the medium direct the finished form of the design, rather than begin with too rigid an objective. In this way the 'thinking hand discovers the thoughts of the material', and the outcome has greater chances of compatibility and harmony.

FIG. 11 *(opposite)*

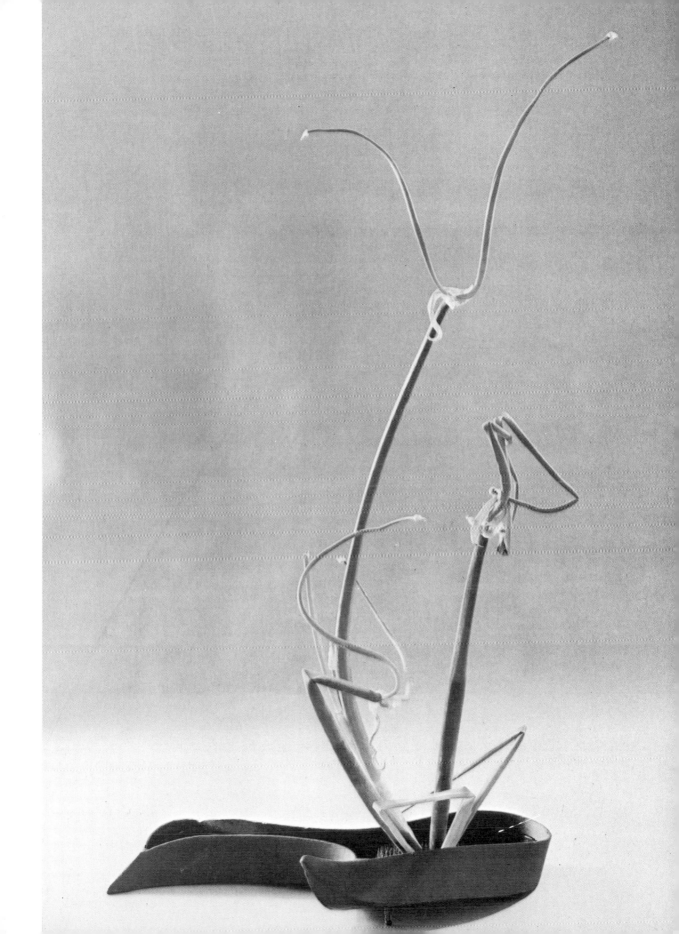

FIG. 12 *(left) and* FIG. 13

4

A NEW LOOK
AT CONTAINERS

The container today does so much more than hold water for the flowers. It can be, and often is, the initial inspiration for an exciting design. Some of the stunning vases available now are stimulating to work with, since they call for an equally imaginative design to balance their distinctive features. The challenge is to make both plant material and container complement one another, to make the one enhance the other.

We are fortunate in that so many vases are now designed with the needs of the flower arranger in mind. So the colour, shape and texture is sympathetic to that of the plant material. This unity should enrich the design.

The more spectacular the vase, the greater the challenge. A very distinctive shape, eye-catching texture or striking colour is exciting, but calls for greater ingenuity in selecting the supporting items. The right combination comes sometimes only after a lot of experimenting. This can be frustrating, but it is better to wait for the right inspiration when one often ends up with a totally different result from the one visualised.

Some containers are more resistant than others. Others are easy to use right from the start and adapt readily to a variety of arrangements. I find the container in Fig. 14 a very accommodating one. The edge of the dish has a very rhythmical line which enhances that of the plant material. Colour and texture are also particularly sympathetic to most plants. It is a pleasant earthy colour which suits both bright and subtle colour harmonies. The texture is rough on the outside, semi-matt on the inside.

Sometimes it is better to compromise and to regard the more unusual vase as a complete art object. It can then be used as the feature or accessory with the design built around it. Again, the right complement of supporting items is needed so that even though the container is the highlight, one appreciates the contribution of the natural material also.

The line and form of the Clive Brooker ceramic in Fig. 15 is so distinctive it would be a pity to camouflage it. I felt that the circular pattern of the wood accentuated its own major rhythm. Line, form, colour and texture of material and container become integrated effectively. The allium seedhead at the top raises the plant material to a more dominant level but does not lessen the impact of the container since it continues and is part of the general rhythm of the whole of the design. It would be very interesting to know what the designer visualised in each creation and whether another artist's interpretation is a surprise or a shock.

The flower arranger who is a potter, or one who can ingeniously create a container from trivia is lucky as each project can be geared to the end objective; the vase can be designed to suit the particular requirement from the start.

The container is part of the design in all types of arrangements, augmenting style or promoting colour or texture interest, but it features more obviously in the very modern or abstract style where the container is frequently an actual part of the line and spatial interest of the design, closely involved in its rhythm and balance and its final form. It makes a greater impact than in the mass arrangement where profusion often hides a lot of the container. Examples of the important role of the container in the design with accent on space and line can be seen and studied throughout the book.

The arranger today can add a touch of originality with a container since there are so many individually styled ones available. No longer are we restricted to the mass-produced, which makes container hunting so much more exhilarating and its use a more imaginative procedure.

I should add that originality is possible with the simplest or cheapest of containers if it happens to benefit the design concept. When materials of dramatic line or colour already provide enough interest, an unpretentious container is often just the right complement.

It is interesting to study the effect of a single arrangement in different containers. It becomes evident from the total effect how much more pleasing certain combinations are than others.

FIG. 14 *(above) and* FIG. 15

5

ARRANGEMENTS IN MODERN SETTINGS

(a) In a modern church

To many, flower arranging means the traditional style. The flowing mass arrangement is much loved; very 'British' where plenty of rain gives masses of foliage to enrich and enlarge a profusion of colours and textures of flowers. It can be very beautiful. But there are settings, times and situations where the sparser, more streamlined group is more compatible.

I would like to tell you of two modern churches where I did a flower demonstration. This will prove I practise what I preach and that I am not forever plodding away with pen and paper just thinking out theories.

The church at Upper Basildon, near Pangbourne in the Thames Valley is in dramatic contrast to its quiet rural setting of apple orchards and green fields. A very tall, distinctive piece of modern architecture — impressive verticals met by sharp diagonals here and there. The apex of one is in bright cerise, which is startling against the white facade.

Inside it is light and spacious. The central portion soars upwards to a huge triangular section of glass and the extreme simplicity of the interior design gives great serenity. Overcrowded, fussy displays would be entirely out of character here. The streamlined setting called for the more restrained decoration. I have never seen a less pretentious altar. A plain rectangle of stone finished in light wood, which made the large wooden cross suspended above all the more compelling.

I had not previously seen the church so was not familiar with the setting. I worked, therefore, on interpreting themes from the Bible, hoping that these would blend with various aspects of the interior. Everything really worked for me. The plain walls, restrained ornamentation and subdued colours showed the arrangements to advantage, whilst the arrangements themselves softened the severity of the setting without detracting from its clean, simple lines.

My two arrangements symbolising 'The Crucifixion' and 'The Resurrection' were placed on the altar. One in a tall stone vase blended with the stone altar, and had three long-stemmed **Baccarat** roses supplemented by very tall cane for an ascending vertical movement. The other, of dark wood, tied in with that of the rough wooden cross. The plain white walls in the background gave tremendous definition to the composition.

The sculptural quality of the beautiful wooden font was complemented by the arrangement interpreting 'The Garden of Eden' (Fig. 16). I used a large piece of twisted wood for 'The Tree of Knowledge of Good and Evil', smooth in texture, matching that of the font. The sharply pointed, twisting strelitzia leaves (dried) suggested the serpent, with gold lilies for beauty and innocence. Green fatsia leaves

and a light green apple set on a light wooden base completed a cream, green and gold scheme. The 'Wedding in Cana' with 'The Turning of Water into Wine' was a large, slightly fuller arrangement, with peach and soft yellow flowers set against large palm and cycas leaves in beige – brown hues, complementing a terra-cotta water carrier from Israel and masses of green and purple grapes. This looked well against the warm brown of the organ.

The sombre tones of blue and purple in 'Darkness was upon the Face of the Deep', on the other hand, needed the light from a side window and a pastel background. Bleached broom was used to create movement on the water in a sleek modern design.

Twisted brown twigs gave a lot of movement and vigour also in 'Christ driving the Money Lenders from the Temple'. This was in bright gold and brown and fitted rather well beside the hymn board on a narrow shelf.

I did make one flowing rather more traditional arrangement to depict 'My Cup runneth over'. But 'Rejoice in the Lord' was carried out in the abstract style with lots of black cane and brilliant red flowers. I did enjoy the challenge and the satisfaction of designing in such a modern setting.

I then went to the church of St. Augustine at Whitchurch, Bristol. This was, if anything, an even more inspiring setting. A superbly designed modern church, incredibly simple in concept, but with all the impact of supreme craftsmanship and artistry. All the interior was in very light stone, and pale blond beechwood. So clean, so light, so spacious, so immaculate. Nothing additional detracted from its two very special features. Firstly, the simple beauty of the long vertical panes of the glass windows with their straight bands of spectrum colours, one in the warm, the other in the cool hues. The church is lit at night, so that these colours can be seen for miles around.

Secondly attention is focused on the magnificent sculpture of 'Christ in Glory' set high in a commanding position above the altar. It is a very modern interpretation, impressive in size and concept and powerfully expressive. What inspiration, but a formidable challenge even to begin to complement in artistry.

This church setting called for bold, sculptural designs; strong, definite lines and clean silhouettes; for restraint and simplicity to complement its architecture. The ornate and the overstated would quarrel with atmosphere and simplicity of concept. Dramatic, modern arrangements on the other hand looked tremendously effective (see Colour Plate 2). The old church was destroyed in the war, so that this church is new in every sense. St. Augustine is ecumenical, striving for church and world unity. It is progressive, forward looking, meeting the needs of today. It is set in a typically un-beautiful new housing estate and caters for all aspects of living. I would love to 'do the flowers' here all the time.

I think it is the consciousness of light and space in the well designed modern church that is so uplifting and sustaining. It is easy to be inspired and to create in such circumstances.

FIG 16 – 'The Garden of Eden' – *A very tall, sparse arrangement of a sculptural nature seemed an appropriate decoration for the area surrounding the wooden font. The driftwood was beautifully sillhouetted against the background (would it distract the eye and mind too much from the sermon?!). The rest of the items were given the same definition: the bold twists of the dried strelitzia leaves stood out sharply, and the gold of the lilies was intensified by the light that streamed in from the window behind. The scope of the setting is quite apparent. It is easy to visualise a number of possibilities that would benefit greatly from its simplicity and from its lighting – ideal for a mobile of angels at Christmas time!*

(b) For the modern home

The clean, simple lines of many of today's homes look well with flower arrangements that echo the simplicity. Many people still prefer a mass of flowers it is true, but for economical and practical reasons, more and more are turning to the sparse, quickly replenished decoration.

To buy a lot of flowers is costly. Many town dwellers have to rely on florist material. Land gets scarcer all the time and some of the newer houses have very small gardens, many just patios with the odd tub or window box. Even those with large gardens find the time and labour involved increasingly difficult.

It is therefore practical and satisfying to be able to use a little for an interesting display, to give full emphasis to the colour, line or texture of the few items used. With a little imagination one can cut out time and labour. A piece of wood, or a branch with a good line, often needs very little extra. The arrangement in Colour Plate 3 can be easily re-constructed. The framework can remain as semi-permanent, and the fresh material can be replaced as available or to suit the occasion. The anthuriums used here for a very special occasion perhaps, with a few roses, lilies, or delphiniums in summer, colourful dahlias in season, and a sprig of greenery or a flowering shrub when flowers are scarce. The swirls of cane bend with the con-tainer in colour and texture, the flowers are highlighted by this harmony. This is a large arrangement which needs to be well displayed against an uncluttered background to give full value to line and space interest. For a smaller area, or a low table, I like the little round pot in Fig. 17. Here again the living material can be quickly changed, with a twist of cane left as background. The arrangement looks nice from all angles.

Long lasting leaves are a good choice for the busy housewife, and foliage arrangements can be very satisfying. A few bold spears of yucca, New Zealand flax or iris, combined with one or two broad leaves like megasea, fatsia and ivy with a sprig of eleagnus or euonymus for added colour perhaps. These all last for ages, and a few drops of bleach will keep the water sweet. Occasionally a more exotic leaf can be spared from a house plant like monstera, ficus, aspidistra, or a strelitzia leaf or two acquired with the flowers from the florist. These leaves are so decorative in themselves they can look dramatic, and the arrangements complete without flowers. A plain wall shows up their interesting shape.

The greatest problem, perhaps, in the modern room is the centrally heated atmosphere which is not very kind to fresh flowers. One cannot expect them to last a very long time. This is where dried material scores since it can stand up to heat and

dryness, needing no attention other than a flick of a feather duster. They are extremely easy to blend in with almost any colour scheme, and can provide beautifully sculptured displays. I rely heavily on them for their durability and bless their labour saving quality. It's the only way I can impress the unexpected caller! They can also be combined with fresh material most effectively. One or two jewel coloured flowers with the mellow browns or greys can be very striking.

It is now possible to buy a lot of imported dried material also, and though this is more expensive initially than preserving or drying your own, it is usually so tough and durable that it lasts indefinitely and very little is needed for dramatic effect. There are also

FIG. 17 *(above)*

some very tastefully coloured items on sale which can tie in with and enhance the general decor.

The home-maker today also has the great asset of a varied choice of containers which can add so much to the artistic effect of a small amount of plant material. There are some excellently designed pots on the market, in glass, metal, synthetics and pottery. Thick, chunky modern glassware in jewel colours can add a lustre and sparkle to a bunch of leaves, or provide the ideal setting for one expensive bloom or a spray of orchids perhaps. There are some wonderful glazings in the pottery range, and lovely, subtle off-beat colourings that can make the ordinary arrangement quite exciting. Sophisticated colours and smart, shining glazes would complement a striking colour scheme used in the home. There are some very good reproductions in fibre glass and other synthetics that are not too expensive.

Better still if you can make your own with style, colour and texture to suit. An interesting individual collection can be built up quite cheaply this way.

Often an ugly pot can be made more beautiful with a new colour or texture. A vase with a rather dominating pattern, can be covered with a mixture of Polyfilla, fine sand and powder paints to make the new surface more compatible with the plant material used and it can always be altered again when necessary. Another method is to paint the surface with a thin layer of glue, then roll this in crushed eggshells, rice or grit. Old bleach bottles, biscuit tins and other household trivia can be transformed this way. Or, of course, an original collection can be acquired more professionally at pottery classes.

A flower arrangement for the home is designed as part of its setting. It is very fulfilling to create something to enhance this which one can enjoy at leisure.

FIG 18 — *An arrangement that, once constructed, looks after itself and makes a bold and spectacular display. It is made up of a blend of dried and preserved material. The cycas leaves dry easily into a pleasant soft yellow, often curling into intriguing shapes. The dark brown of the lotus pods makes a good contrast of colour — further accentuated by the light beige of the bamboo leaf fans. These add a note of gaiety and extra rhythm, like the swish of a dancer's skirt..The preserved plants are Monkey Puzzle (Arucaria). I know they dry easily, but preserved they have a richer colour and are softer to handle. A few preserved fatsia leaves give a contrast of form and texture. The stoneware container is in brown and beige and comes from the Jersey potteries.*

6

CHANGING STYLES

Style evolves in a personal and a general way. In the broader context, it is possible to compare various styles for their distinctive characteristics. It is interesting also to note certain emphases and trends, common to all the arts at one given time, and their particular application to the medium of flower arrangement. This does not necessarily mean that there is one particular style belonging to any one period, as style is infinitely variable, and the characteristics of one often merge into another.

The mass arrangement never seems to lose general appeal and popularity. This, in its more controlled design form, is often called 'Line-mass', as its underlying structure is based on a definite geometric shape, like the cone or the pyramid. It is neat, compact, with colours and textures methodically grouped. Each part is unified for overall rhythm, the line presenting the final form and movement of the arrangement. The line-mass arrangement could be said to mark the breakaway from the more amorphous, loose, flowing · mass arrangements which preceded them; a firmer structural discipline becomes evident and colours and shapes are more sharply defined. The principle relates to Cubism, with its discipline of form and design based on classical geometry.

Colour Plate 4 is an example of an arrangement with line-mass characteristics. Line, ·though not pronounced, can easily be defined and presents the final form of a neat, triangular design. Colours are purposely grouped for a definite line of movement. Geometry enters into the form of the mass.

Fig. 19 shows a design moving nearer the more definite 'Line' arrangement, where line becomes the dominant feature. Line becomes more accentuated, often made dramatic. Material used becomes sparser, so as not to hide the line, as seen in Fig. 20 where it has unquestionably become the major interest of the design.

The very stylised line arrangements based on a crescent shape, Hogarth curve, sections of a triangle and so on, when very rigidly contrived, can have a certain stiffness of form. Materials used are often coaxed into curves and angles to form a very 'accurate' line for a sophisticated pattern, which can be rather hard. Often line can be modified and softened by developing rhythms more in keeping with the natural line of the plants. The arrangement in Fig. 21 is an easy flowing line design, where the natural line of the palm spathes is used for a smooth rhythm. The dried palm leaves carry their own movement in their radiating lines, but their placement in the design blends their rhythm with that of the spathes for a soft unified movement throughout.

By studying the line of the material and letting its natural rhythm of growth guide the shape of the design, the result is often a 'free', less geometric shape. Free form is often the term applied to such arrangements that do not readily fit into the more stylised L-shape, crescent or Hogarth curve.

These can be rather satisfying designs, often with the grace and appeal of a natural form. Each is really a law unto itself, since it does not conform to a set pattern. They are a refreshing change from the more repetitive, easily categorised shape. The branch in Fig. 22 has such an interesting shape it is satisfying enough on its own, combined with a sympathetic container, or with a rosette — like a spray of *Mahonia bealii*, which again has a beautiful enough line and form to be displayed 'as is'. The free-form style is a logical break-away from stiff stylised designing, hence the popularity of 'Landscape' type arrangements. It is not strictly a style as such, since obviously a landscape can be created in any style. In flower arranging this category is associated with a 'naturalistic' type of design, with the materials placed in as 'natural' a way as possible to suggest a scene from Nature. The aim is to give an impression of a vista rather than to build up a strong design pattern or a conventional arrangement. A series of placements in different planes suggests a desert scene in Fig. 25 whilst items placed at varying heights convey a larger vista in Fig. 24.

FIG 19 — This arrangement is based on a triangular form, but here the accent on space is much more pronounced. The plant material used is sparser, with each item clearly outlined in space. Line interest is therefore more dramatic and dominant. The twisted honeysuckle vines make a lively, rhythmical outline; the empty areas add depth and additional movement; and the line made by the placement of the round flowers sets up a further rhythm with the monstera leaves, thus increasing the overall effect.

FIG 20 — *Line is clearly the major interest of this design. Every unit is so placed as to maximise its effect. The eye moves effortlessly along the structure of the slender twigs, over their exciting and varied rhythms. The poppy flower serves to reinforce, rather than interrupt, the movement. So does the base through repetition of line and colour. Line used effectively can acquire tremendous appeal and power as an element. Designers in all spheres are well aware of its expressive possibilities. A plain, contrasting background of appropriate dimensions adds clarity and definition to this design.*

FIG 21 — *A line design need not necessarily look hard and stylised. If one follows the natural line of the material an easy flowing rhythm can emerge. The palm spathes in the arrangement here have a most beautiful line, and this establishes the form of the design. The gentle curve of the two at the top form a smooth movement, whilst the lower spathes with the more dramatic line add extra vigour and depth. The clipped palm leaves continue the motion, already determined by the spathes, but their own structure carries separate rhythms. There are various lines, but all work for a unified movement. Harmony of colour and texture in material and container maintains an easy flow from one to the other.*

FIG 22 — *With plants of distinctive line and shape, it is easy to let them direct the finished form of the arrangement. The items used in this arrangement would not be easy to force into a pattern other than one which follows their natural line. The combination of these rhythms gives a smooth sequence to the design, but the natural flow of the material is still maintained. This gives the composition a rather free, casual quality.*

FIG 23 — *In this composition using two containers the form of the design is dictated by the line of the dried twigs. Their varied directional movements make interesting patterns of space, and the rhythms created carry the eye to wide dimensions. The roses are nicely encompassed within the framework. Interest here is created with very little material, and that of a kind often overlooked. Shrubs like rhododendron often have a mass of dried growth at their base. I am always collecting these, as I find they help to create a three-dimensional quality without overpowering the design. They are also easy to fix into the mechanics and take up very little room in a small container or pinholder.*

FIG 24 — *The landscape arrangement is very popular. It appeals possibly through its evocative quality, recalling or suggesting a natural scene. It presents the familiar and well loved in nature. Often very little is needed to conjure up a vivid picture. By scaling the various items to create impressions of different heights, a larger vista is conjured up — a branch to interpret a tall tree with small flowers growing underneath or succulents, stones, mosses and fungi at ground level. Again, tall, spear-like leaves and stems around a pool of water with a suitable figurine or other accessories would create an easily imagined scene. Placements in different planes give a greater vista of depth and distance. Rocks and knobbles of wood representing mountain peaks can be placed one behind the other. Some items placed forward, some at the rear in separate placements suggest a larger panorama.*

FIG 25 — *With this you must imagine the Sahara desert: sparse vegetation, rocks and sand, with the occasional oasis for a touch of green, living material (the 'Palm' is a stem of* Cyperus alterni folius). *The 'rocks' here are authentic Sahara products, collected by my elder son (my family are well trained!). They are called 'Les Roses du Sable', and are formed by the crystallisation of sand particles into formations resembling the petals of a rose, though pictured here they tend to look like miniature Daleks!*

Abstract

In great contrast to the naturalistic are abstract designs, which are not the faithful copying of nature, though they can originate from sensitive observation of the natural world. Abstract art, and abstract flower arrangements, do not appeal to everyone. Many find the non-realistic presentation meaningless, others more attuned to the aims of abstractionism delight in the chances it offers to design more freely. To me, it seems a natural evolvement from a growing appreciation of the beauty of design, and an opportunity to use the medium differently.

An abstract arrangement should not be evaluated against traditional work, since it differs totally in intent. It should be considered as yet another facet of designing, more suitable with some plant items than others. Many are confused by the word abstract, as it has many different connotations. When plant material is used to create line, to define space, to build a geometric shape, it is not being used naturally but abstractly. The arranger chooses the material and its characteristics for designing purposes, so there is a degree of abstractionism in most *designed* arrangements.

But when the technique is stressed and developed for its own sake, an abstract is generally taken to mean a definite style which differs from the 'Free-Style' or the Modern'. In this context, the material is used in a way so far removed from its natural associations that it becomes pure shape, line or form; a texture or colour sensation. It functions without its growth implications, it starts and ends with itself. The further away from the natural, the more abstract the presentation.

Since there is no need to portray nature realistically, as in traditional work, the arranger can design with full creative liberty, cutting loose from conventional, set formulae, to design in a more personal way, simplifying, condensing and refining for the most effective presentation.

For full emphasis and import the material is used in any way that suits the designer's purpose. It may be altered in appearance by being dyed, bleached, stripped, painted etc., or it may be knotted, twisted, or manipulated into a new form. Placements and usage can be wholly non-realistic. This, obviously, is more feasible and practical with some plant material than others. The dried or the preserved is easier to manipulate, and the more unnatural placements are easier without the need to have the stems in water as with the fresh.

Certain plants lend well to creating new forms, like reeds, reedmace, fresh bamboo stalks, strap leaves like those of iris, or the foliage of reedmace. Their natural form is altered in Figs. 26, 27 and 28 to make geometric patterns. The designs are austere, with everything reduced to essentials — there is no attempt to depict natural growth habits. The lysitichum and the yellow iris in Figs. 27 and 28 are merely emphasis points with added colour and texture.

This type of abstract arrangement is generally categorised as non-objective or decorative. The relationship of line with space is the subject, and the appeal lies mainly in a certain preciseness and sense of order, which can be serene and restful. It is perhaps rather impersonal, unemotional one might say, or not romantic. Much of the unity and visual appeal depends on a finely balanced pattern.

The arrangements in Fig. 29 and Colour Plate 5 are based on a theme, and are therefore more compositional and expressive. The subject however, is not realistically portrayed and may convey something quite different to you, the viewer. Instead of using the material merely to create shapes and areas of space, it is now used symbolically to express my feelings about a subject. To make the meaning as clear and forceful as possible, the statement is simplified and only what is important to the interpretation is included. I am not being literal as in traditional interpretive work using realistic props and details, as the aim is to suggest a quality apart from the actual or the real, the essence rather than the outward appearance of the subject. The ragged texture of the bark in Colour Plate 5 is used to interpret the destructive element in nature. Erosion or corrosion is conveyed in the line and form of the design. The height proportions are purposely exaggerated, and the balance given a precarious quality. The line and form of the container repeating that of the plant material strengthens the theme.

The arrangement in Fig. 29 has been built around a subject also, called 'Falling Star'. Material here has been painted for added emphasis. Cane, twisted into varying shapes and blackened, makes a rhythmic space pattern. The line and flow must be kept smooth otherwise the cane tends to look like tangled knitting! Varying the shapes of the cane prevents monotony in the space pattern. This design relies heavily on a feeling of space and movement, which should be made as interesting and forceful as possible. The seedheads of agapanthus and hogweed have been silvered for a shimmering effect against the black. Interpretation is effected with their non-realistic placements, possible because the plants are in their dried stage.

Sometimes, some of the material in a design is used in a non-realistic way; then items are added, perhaps for added colour or texture or further interest, and these are often placed in the more conventional pattern. Something has been 'added to' the essentials in these instances, which makes the design semi-realistic, not a true abstract.

Many people prefer this

approach with its touch of the familiar in much the same way as some prefer a semi abstract painting or sculpture, where the image is only slightly lost and where there is a hint of the recognisable.

In the examples that follow, you can see how the material in each one has been chosen for its contribution to the design pattern, to create its line, to control the areas of space, and to shape its final form. When the three are compared in terms of an abstract design, clearly Fig. 30 is the least abstract, with its realistic accessories, detail and the realistic use of the plant material. The arrangement in Fig. 31 is a more simplified presentation with a stronger design emphasis. The flowers are still conventionally placed, adding colour and texture to that of line and space. The design in Fig. 32 is the most abstract, as here all is reduced to the design structure; it is merely the interplay of line, form space — the pure or the essential form without the detail.

Once the plant material is appreciated as a design force rather than its role in Nature, its essential character can be used expressively. The arranger can respond to its 'gesture' — to the inner quality or essence — as expressed in its line, form, colour or texture.

I have tried to emphasise the expressive qualities of the wood sculptures in Fig. 33 and Fig. 34 with suitable complementary material. Each has a distinctive form and character. The one in Fig. 33 is a very suave shape, with a smooth, polished surface. It has a dynamic rhythm, which I aimed to capture with the movement of the willow and cane looped into vigorous lines. Their smooth texture accents that of the wood. Strength, vigour, and flamboyant movement seem the essence to abstract in this instance.

The other piece in Fig. 34 invites a different response. It has a more jagged, angular line and sharper contours evoking a different rhythm to that of the smoothly flowing, curved lines of the other sculpture. It has great interest of texture with roughness predominating. These qualities are echoed in the zig-zag pattern of the thorns and their angular line. It is difficult to be totally abstract in flower arrangement, since the medium consists of recognisable items. We are experimenting within these limitations, and in the context of a design technique, i.e. that of using plant material in a non realistic way.

FIG. 26 *(opposite)*

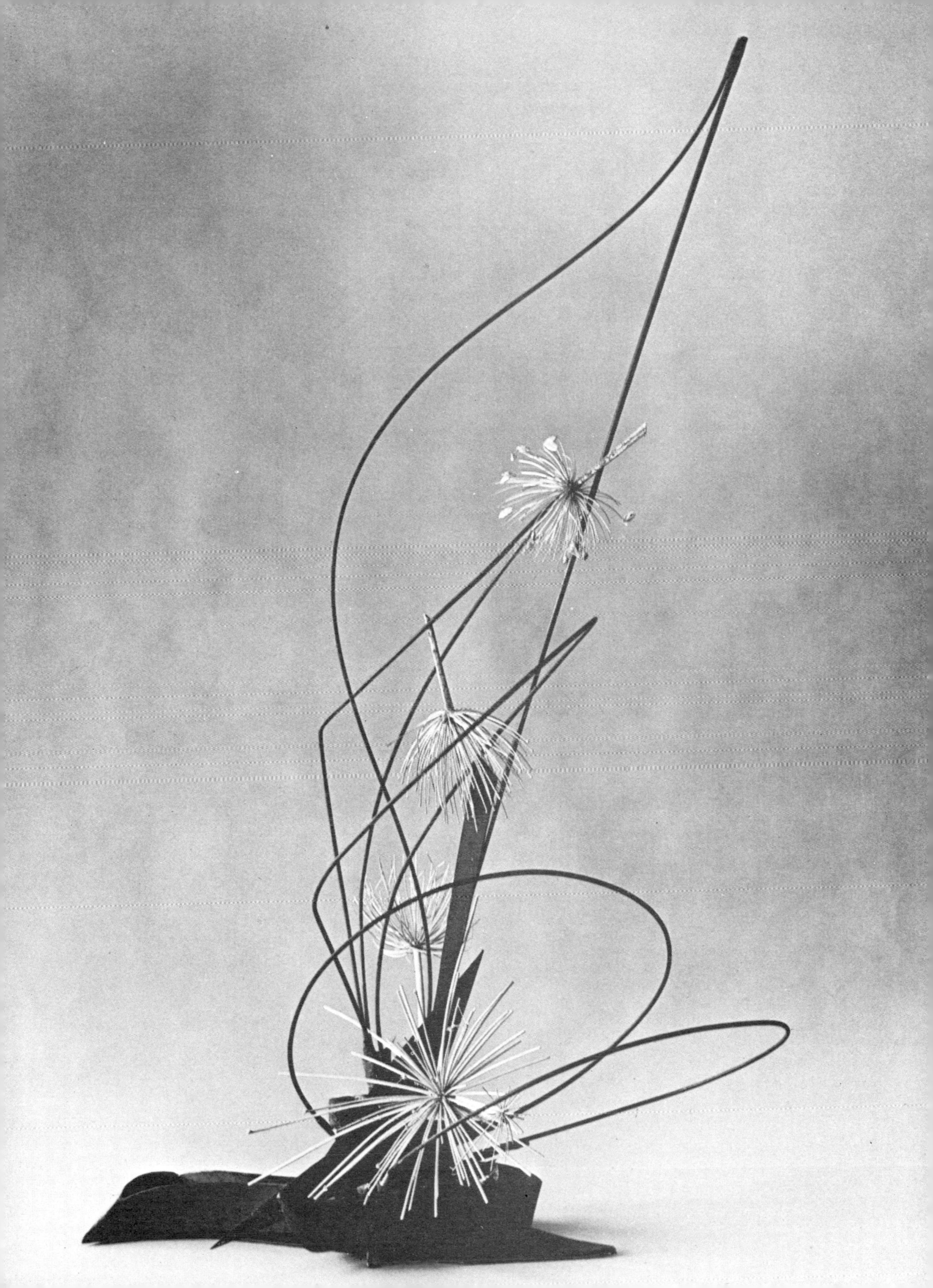

FIG 30 — *A fairly realistic interpretation, with music or rhythm as its theme. Clearly, the strength of the interpretation lies in the rhythmic quality of the design. A buoyant movement is set up by the swirls of black-painted cane. This is supported by the line of the gerbera flowers and croton leaves, whose colour and gaiety, combined with harmonious accessories, promote the suggestion of a rich, vibrant musical beat.*

FIG 31 — *A more restrained presentation than that on the previous page, and one not quite so realistically portrayed. In this design too the nature of the theme is conveyed in line, form, and colour. It has a more delicate air, suggestive of the strings, perhaps, rather than the beat of the drums. Colour, form, and texture are correspondingly softer and lighter. It is lyrical rather than dramatic.*

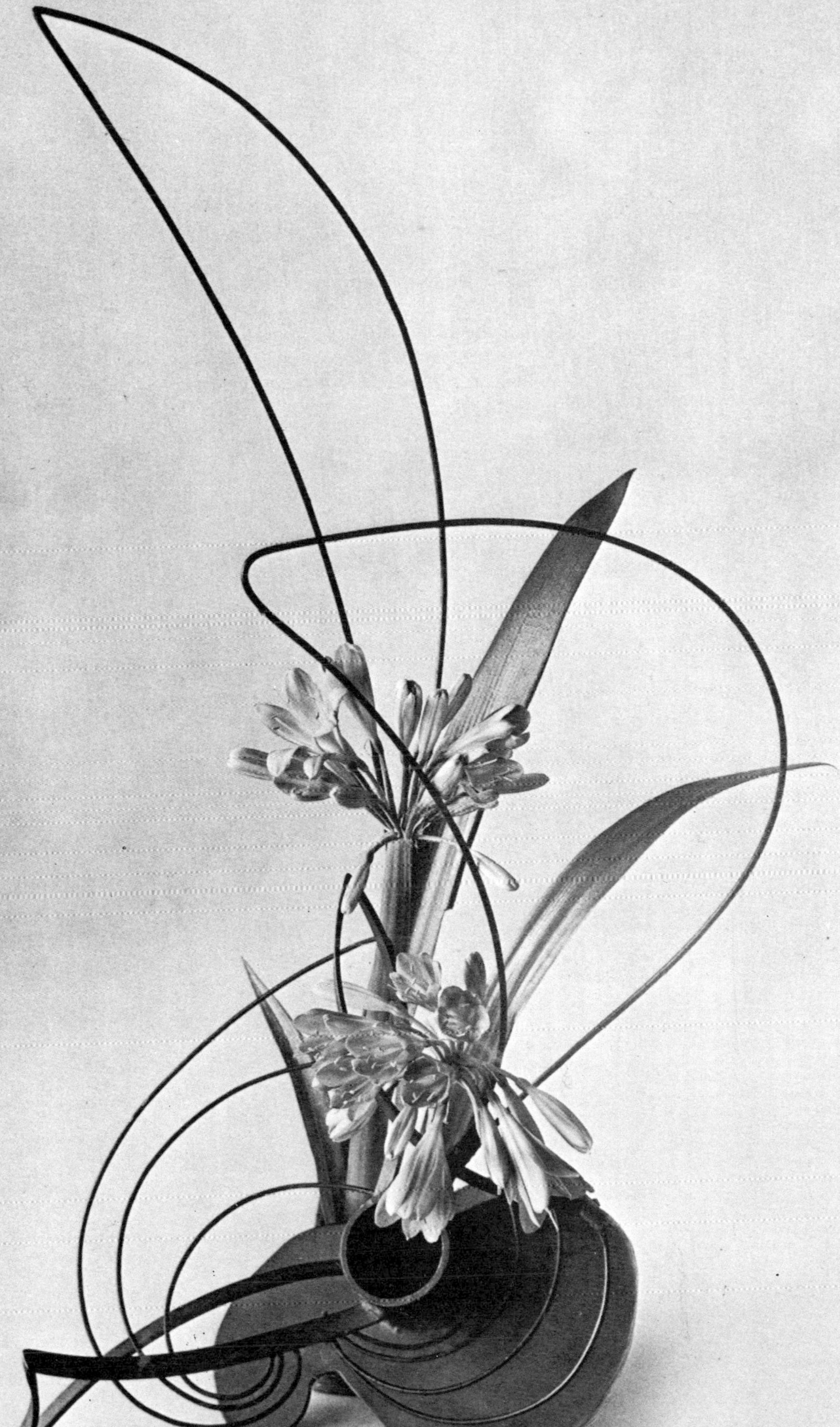

FIG 32 — *The theme of music
presented in an abstract design.
Here all is reduced to line and
pattern, without the details.
Strong rhythm is communicated
by the line of the twisted salix
twigs, continued by the cane,
and picked up by the pattern
of the metal container. There is
a contrast of note in the
bleached wisteria vine and the
preserved magnolia leaves in
the background. Crescendo is
suggested by the second black
wrought-iron container used as
a base.*

FIG. 33 *(left) and* FIG. 34

NON-REALISTIC ACCESSORIES

Realistic accessories have been used in flower arranging for a long time. They are useful in extending interest and furthering a theme, the effective ones adding an extra touch of realism and conviction.

When needed in abstract or semi-abstract composition they must support the non-realistic presentation. They will therefore not be realistic copies and need not represent anything recognisable. They can, like the 'natural' accessory, enrich the theme or improve the design pattern and are the same challenge to use well.

For comparison I have used a realistic figure (Fig. 35). To make the composition look as 'natural' or as 'real' as possible a naturalistic setting was created, using the material to resemble natural growth as closely as possible. One can imagine a woodland glade with a pool and a cool white figure in a serene pose. It has a straightforward story-telling quality.

In contrast the 'figure' in Fig. 36 is not a wholly recognisable one. It has a suggestion of realism though the image would probably vary with the individual. To me it looks like a witch with a broomstick and I have tried to build up around this idea. The design is not conventional, however, as I wanted to accent the suggestive rather than the realistic characteristics. The plant material is used in a non-natural way, with the willow twigs tied to form a pattern. The spaces balance and contrast with the solid areas and keep the design buoyant. Slight contrast of texture and a further accent to the theme is added with a tuft of dried bamboo leaves. The 'witch' is fashioned from a piece of wood.

The accessory in Fig. 37 is totally abstract in concept. Carved again from natural wood, it is a much more impressive and dramatic item than the smaller sculpture. Being rather complete in itself it is difficult to combine it successfully with additional material. I have merely created space and movement around it so as not to hide or confuse its strong form. The strong sculptural line of the honey-suckle vine repeats that of the wood, emphasising curves and hollows. By creating space and movement the sculpture is now seen in greater depth and the open pattern of the vine contrasts with the smooth, suave and compact form of the wood. The reeds also through contrast of line help to vitalise the design and make us more conscious of the spaces created by the sculptural nature of the different items.

The abstract wood shape in Fig. 38 is combined with other abstract forms to interpret 'Thunder and Lightning'. The stripped ivy twigs give strong, swift, irregular movement, complementing that of the accessory. Hardboard shapes, painted a dull black, contrast in form, colour and texture to emphasise the qualities of the light, smooth wood. Lack of harmony between accessory and the rest of the materials is just as disastrous in abstract as traditional work, even more so if anything, because of the simplified presentation of the abstract and its elimination of details.

A realistic object is perhaps easier to use, since it has the familiarity of associations, making it easier to compose around it with materials suitable to its nature, character or activities. A fisherman figure would suggest water plants; a wood carver, woody materials; a farmer, grasses and harvest items and so on. With an object less readily associated with reality one relies entirely on form, line, colour or texture, or a feeling or atmosphere induced by the item.

The figurine in Fig. 35 presented no great problem in association. It should be pointed out, however, that even in this naturalistic style, there is a degree of abstraction, in that the material is taken out of its natural setting and used to suggest something else. But the presentation is more realistic than in the other examples.

FIG. 35 *(left) and* FIG. 36

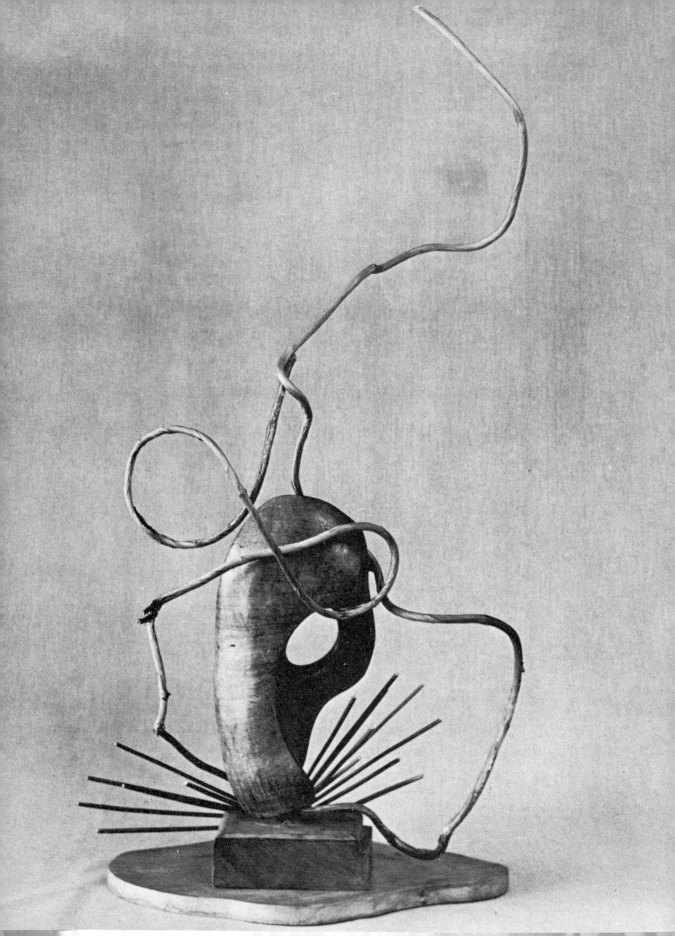

FIG. 37 *(left) and* FIG. 38

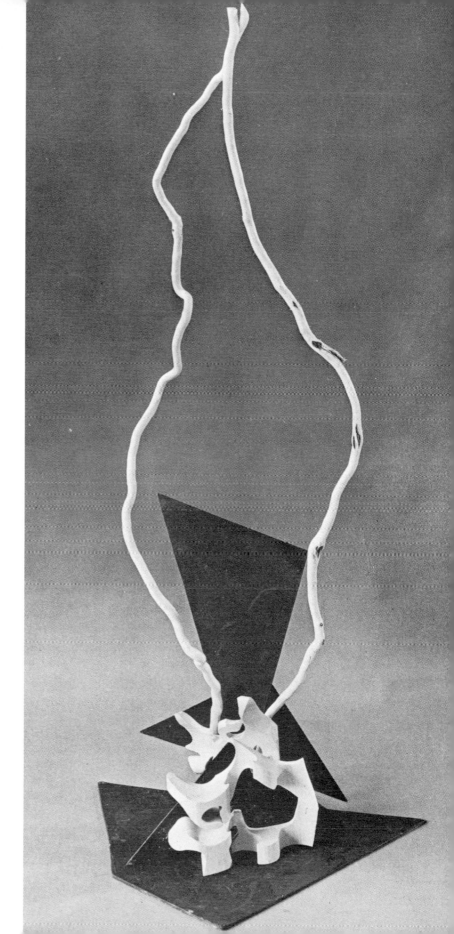

THE INFLUENCE
OF OTHER ARTS

There is often a similarity of concept in the different arts. In certain instances a modern sculpture and painting share techniques which make it difficult to say what province the work really belongs to. The artist in each instance has introduced methods and materials alien to the traditional concepts. The paintings of today show montages of materials like glass and paper, string, sand, layers of hessian and other objects that add interesting textures. The methods used are just as unconventional, with the dripping, splashing, throwing or spraying of paints. These are new approaches by those who want to get away from conventional usage, and who have come to regard painting as an object in itself rather than a representation of something else.

The modern sculptor also makes use of wire, string, perspex, metal and 'found objects', using again methods foreign to the traditions of sculptors of the past. With transparent materials like plastic and stainless steel, space is defined by constructing rather than by carving or modelling.

Twentieth century art shows tremendous activity. It also shows great liberty of expression, with the artist free to express in whatever way his vision dictates.

It is feasible to have the same enthusiasm in flower arranging. We too are continually extending into new directions and are as keen to develop our art as other artists. It is stimulating to seek new techniques and to use new items, to move into new dimensions.

Just as the student of painting is encouraged to splash, dribble and play about with paint, to use sponges and knives and old socks for special effects of texture, to try out the marvellous new colours and paints available, so the student of flower arranging should have the chance to experiment with the medium as much as possible.

Interesting developments keep emerging and we now see some very exciting innovations at major shows which cause both controversy and great interest.

With growing appreciation of design, arranging techniques continue to change. The more keenly the arranger sees the materials of flower arranging as design units, the more she will experiment with the designing possibilities. As in the other arts new ways of expression will therefore continue to appear, as ever more effective methods of using the medium are discovered. Designs will show greater liberty in the move away from the conventional pattern.

(a) Collage and montage

A grouping of non-floral objects like that in Fig. 39 is similar to the collage or the montage in painting. It is a composition of items with interesting texture and shape (cork, bark, floats and seaweed) arranged artistically.

Dark and light areas give a degree of movement to relieve the flat 2D nature of the 'picture'. Textures vary from smooth to very coarse pitted surfaces, which I at least find very attractive. Since the natural here has been altered into man-made objects, the construction extends beyond the realm of natural flora — certainly beyond 'flower' arranging.

This is so in the other 'picture' also (Fig. 40), though here natural plant material is used, but in an altered state to make an abstract pattern. Dried reeds are bent to create new shapes, then arranged in a pleasing, orderly sequence. The light and dark backgrounds create a little depth. This rather precise mathematical style will not appeal to those who like a soft flowing and more evocative style. The approach is intellectual rather than emotional perhaps, but I find it a rather satisfying mental exercise. It does take patience to make a rhythmic, visually pleasing pattern and I juggled quite a lot with those triangles. You might be amused to know I was shockingly backward at geometry in school. Perhaps I am a late developer and this is my way of making amends.

Looking at the modern paintings often referred to as 'abstract classic' or 'hard edge', where the edges of colour are clean-cut, not blended, helps one to appreciate the intention in this style. The sense of order perhaps, and the rhythm and beauty of design through colour. Sometimes the picture looks just as good upside down or sideways, since the design itself is the feature, the subject. If a collage of more free-form shapes is preferred, there are many suitable items like dried or skeletonised leaves, bark of all kinds, fungi, coral, sea fern and a host of other interesting shapes. An example is the other collage (Colour Plate 6), which is a collection of the more amorphous shapes found in nature — fantastic shapes and textures, don't you think? Look at the skeletonised opuntia with its incredibly beautiful and intricate skeletal structure, and the bark of silver birch which also has great textural interest, with variations of surface effect to give light and dark areas. To stress these textures the background was roughened up with Polyfilla paste mixed with sand, washed over with powder paints in black, brown and orange.

I wonder if it is the ephemeral nature of a flower arrangement that leads the arranger to seek a more permanent record of her artistic efforts. A plaque, swag or a picture made with dried material can be enjoyed over a far longer period than a fresh flower arrangement and repays the extra time and labour taken in construction. Flower arrangers have now grown very skilled in this type of work, and there have been magnificent examples of swags that look like the wood

carvings of Grinling Gibbons; and pictures of exquisite colourings made with dried flowers. A more modern version can be made using the material in an abstract pattern, for interest of line, form, colour or texture. Sawing bits of woody stalks and glueing this together is not everyone's idea of a perfect pastime for a rainy afternoon, but it becomes absorbing as patterns emerge and an idea takes shape.

I have used dried polygonum stems in Fig. 41 mainly, with those of hogweed (the lighter colour) for variation of colour here and there; I just doodled with shapes until the result pleased me. By cutting the stems to various lengths and grouping light and darker values, an absolutely flat effect was avoided. It was not planned to represent anything specific, but it might suggest something to you.

FIG. 39

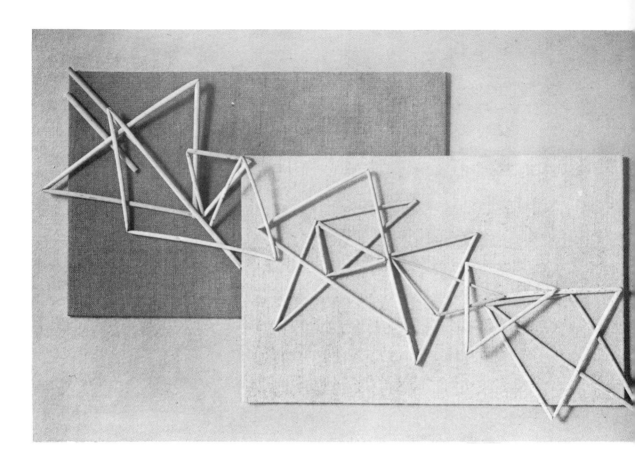

FIG. 40 *(above)*

FIG 41 — *A collage gives the designer greater plasticity and scope for manipulation than a conventional arrangement, where one is working from a single point of radiation. The different parts can be moved about on the flat surface until the right combination is achieved. Here — stems of polygonum and hogweed were shifted around until a pleasing pattern emerged. The different values of light and dark increase the textural interest and rhythm of this decorative relief.*

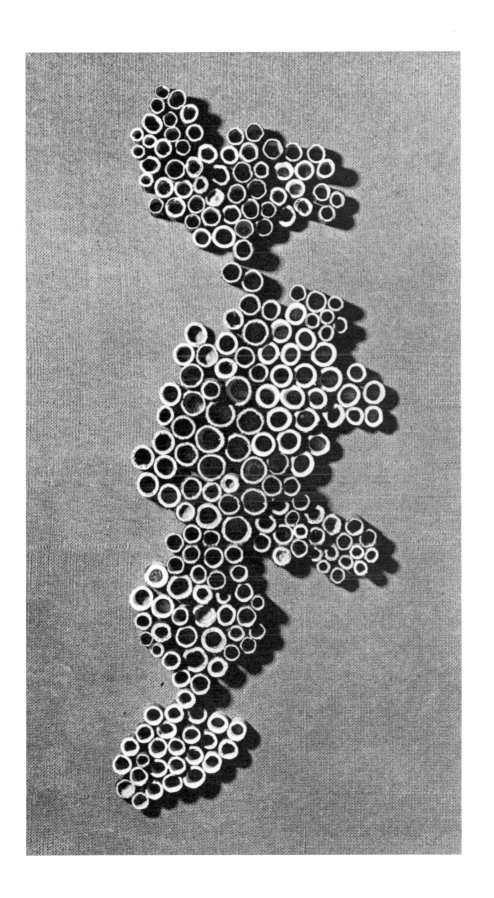

(b) Natural Sculpture
(1) With dried materials.

The overlapping of the arts of flower arranging and that of sculpture is becoming increasingly evident in many modern designs.

Not all our natural plants lend easily to being moulded and manipulated, so items more amenable to change are a more natural choice for creating these sculptural effects.

Wood, in all its varying forms and stages is especially suitable. It is a medium that has been used in flower arranging for a long time. With its natural affinity to flowers and leaves it marries well with these, lending extra interest and often a dramatic quality to an ordinary arrangement.

Not every piece needs the complement of other plant material though. Some have sufficient interest and variety in their own structure to be featured as natural sculpture needing perhaps just the right container or base to accent its special features.

It is more rewarding still to produce a wood sculpture one has worked upon for a special finish. It becomes a more personal product and it calls for greater ingenuity to turn a rather ugly piece into something more alluring.

The piece in Fig. 42 was to start with an old oak stump, soaked in rain water for weeks to loosen all the soft wood. All this messy, pulpy wood was hacked away to reveal the hard healthy wood underneath. This has a most attractive texture, full of holes and hollows which could be lightly polished, though I have left it as a matt surface for the present. The container here adds to the textural interest; it has a wonderful bark-like finish, so is sympathetic in nature to the wood. The rough ivy twigs give a contrast of texture and add further interest of line and space to the composition. The variation of brownish hues in wood and container are very satisfying.

It is also fun to build up a wood sculpture with several pieces of wood, using the same principles of balance, proportion, rhythm and contrast as in a flower arrangement. I have used five separate bits in Fig. 43, all have the same lovely silver-grey colour that wood from the Scottish lochs always seems to have. There is a lot of texture variation — some pieces have a silken smoothness, others are rough and knobbly. All were combined for an interesting pattern of space and line by building up one shape on another with the larger, heavier piece at the base. Each was fixed to the next with strong adhesive. The container blends in colour and texture, and its strong, square line gives a pleasing balance without spoiling the rhythm of the wood. The sculpture has enough variety, contrast and interest, so needs nothing additional. It looks very dramatic against the black wall of my studio.

The sculpture in Fig. 44 was built up in a similar way. This time with more intricate pieces of stripped ivy wood. These have been varnished to bring out all the texture variations and to give a rich honey brown colour. The pot has the same texture and colour with a semi-shiny glaze so that wood and container feature as a whole, and it is not just wood stuck in a pot.

I think using wood this way is very exciting and has great possibilities for the flower arranger interested in extending into natural sculpture. The material lends admirably to such development; wood sculptures make interesting features in the home, since they are durable and as permanent as one wishes. They also have the fascination of something unique. No two pieces of wood are alike. Above all I think they score over the manufactured item because of their natural quality. They have all the interest, variety and beauty of nature's objects.

Many dried items other than wood are excellent for sculptural compositions. I found the palm spathes in Fig. 45 most inspiring for moulding into a suave form. Each individual piece is beautifully sculptured with a bold definite line. I experimented with each in different positions for the most dynamic combination, until the final form was rhythmic and balanced. There is subtle texture variation to give a pleasing light and shade effect. This is further strengthened by a rough pottery base, and a smooth polished stone. The subdued colour through-out gives full emphasis to the drama of line and space.

What fascinating things there are in the plant world. Nature's tiny miracles. Half the fun of flower arranging is in collecting all these treasures which add an exotic touch, and bring back many memories of their happy hunting. The spathes (Fig. 45) were acquired in Malta where I spent a very stimulating week teaching and lecturing. They were picked when fresh, from the cemetery of all places, which seemed to be the Mecca of all the Malta club flower arrangers for plant material.

The agave spears (Fig. 46) were also gathered with the same enthusiasm, off the hot sunny slopes of the Pyrenees. I shall never forget the sight of a small forest of these enormous spears, some five feet high or more. It was the lower leaves, dried to the most fabulous colour and texture that attracted me most. It was murder coping with the vicious spikes, but I managed to win a few that have been much used ever since, so it was worth all the agony. They are a beautiful cream, beige and brown colour. Some dried in a sort of paisley pattern and the shapes are very sculptural.

Plant material is assembled in yet another way in Fig. 47 again resembling modern sculpture, or it could be described as a construction with natural material. The emphasis is on an interesting variation of texture in dried cow-parsley stalks. In using the material this way, its special characteristics are

brought more closely to our
notice. Even in a non-realistic
presentation, basic principles
are observed. A variety of
rhythms is created by light
and dark, and varying directional movements to avoid
total flatness and monotony.
The Gill Drury container has
the right complementary,
sculptural and textural quality. It gives a pleasing balance,
and hides the mechanics
efficiently without reducing
the rhythm of the design.

Colour Plate 7 shows a
similar construction with a
sculptural quality, but with
emphasis more on line that
texture. The reeds are lighter
in form and give a more
delicate appearance suggestive
of fine steel wire sculptures.
Because of the lesser variation
of texture here, the depth
element is not as noticeable.
The advancing colour of the
flowers helps to break up the
flatness and gives greater
definition to the surface. The
attractive container adds
further interest of form,
colour and texture, but is not
too heavy in visual impact to
detract from the buoyancy of
the design.

We might well see 'A
Construction with Natural
Plant Material' as a class title
of a show in the future. It has
exciting possibilities.

FIG. 42 *(opposite)*

FIG. 43 *(left) and* FIG. 44

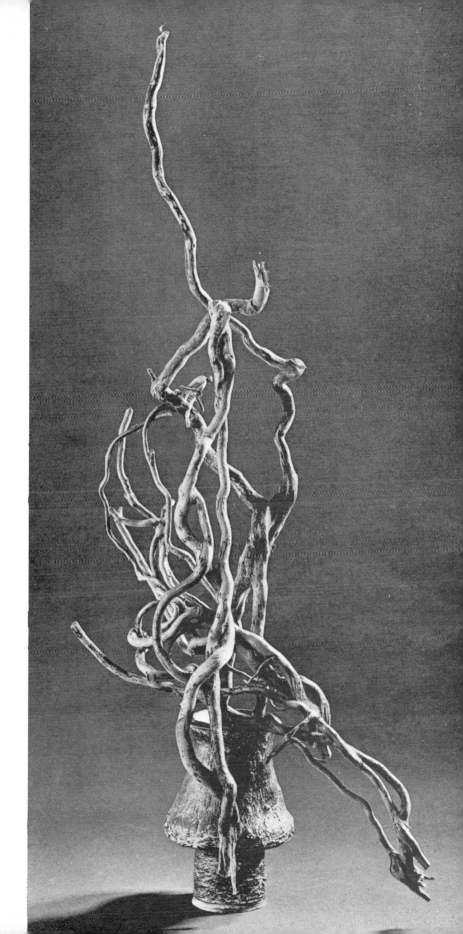

FIG 45 — *In this composition there is an attempt to create the depth and movement typical of sculpture. A flat pattern is static; a three-dimensional structure can be dynamic. A good sculpture will induce us to look at it all round, to experience its form to the full. It is then that one comes to appreciate the meaning of the concept. Inner and outer volumes in this design invite contemplation, while the hollows become an active part of the effect of the design. The contrast of the concave and convex aspects of the material gives vitality to the 'sculpture' and a pleasing visual effect.*

FIG 46 — *Compactness of form in material and in the design structure gives this arrangement a strong, sculptural quality. The agave spears look as though they have been carved and hollowed out. Design depth is increased by the turning of the spears in different directions and by the spaces made by the lower curled up specimens. A blending of form and texture of container with material gives a pleasing unity and strengthens the sculptural effect. The 'feel' of a form, its roundness, its solidity, is an essential attribute.*

FIG. 47

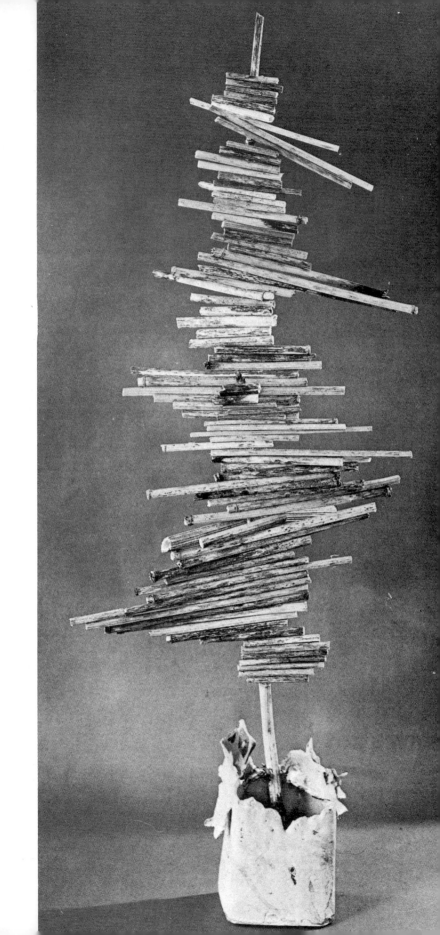

(2) With fresh materials.

We have seen how the dried lends easily to sculptural effects. Let us now look at some fresh items that can be used for similar effects. Many strap leaves are flexible enough to bend into curves. The dracaena leaves in the design in Fig. 49 is an example. With these straight 2D items it is possible to create a structure with a lot of depth and movement to make exciting curves and hollows and a beautifully rhythmic pattern. This is not always easy and it may take time to achieve just the right balance and movement, and of course the mechanics problem is greater. Here, with living plants, the stems need moisture, so the mechanics are bulkier. The solid block of oasis had to be covered without interrupting the natural flow of the design. The last thing one wants is the obvious camouflage.

The problem is easier with the design in Fig. 48 as the mechanics (a pinholder) are hidden entirely by the container. This is a sharper, more vertical composition than the other, which relies on curves and a circular motion. The material is variegated New Zealand flax *(Phormium tenax)* which has a lovely architectural quality, bold, strong and very beautiful. They have been split along the central vein to give greater depth, movement and variety, but the main impression I wanted to create was a strong upward line, to stress their essential characteristics.

In all these sculptural constructions, the complement of container must assist the line and form of the material. The strong, square and precise line of the one used here emphasises that of the flax.

Yucca leaves have a bold strong line too, tougher and more difficult to bend than the flax. Their slightly concave surfaces are ridged in places, giving an attractive frilly effect when cut across. By angling these in a forward line a greater three dimensional effect is created, and more variety in the pattern of the structure. These tough leaves last extremely well when cut, and all sections of their structure are interesting. There is the very fleshy, light coloured portion where the leaf joins the stem of the plant which can be used as a separate feature, with the broad part uppermost. The spike at the top gives a spear-like effect, useful in interpretive work or for design emphasis.

Reeds or sedges are among the most useful items for abstract work. Their straight, uncomplicated structure is very easy to bend or to loop into new patterns, or they can be used straight for line and movement. With such versatility one can spend hours playing with triangles of all shapes and sizes and fitting these together into ever-varying patterns — creating space, altering line until a pleasing balance of the two is achieved. It is fascinating if you like that sort of thing, and they are common and plentiful enough for one to experiment with and discard and start again. They dry well and will even take up a glycerine and water solution if you want to preserve them into a more pliable form. Colour Plate 8 shows a sculptural composition using all three items. Here in colour the depth, movement and variation in hue can be appreciated more fully than in a black and white picture.

FIG. 48 *(see text)*

FIG 49 – *In this example a sculptural pattern is made by manipulating the material into a new form. The natural curves of the dracaena are exaggerated and made more emphatic. A new structure is created that is in keeping with the nature of the material and is originally inspired by it. The essential characteristics are, if anything, emphasised by this treatment. The pattern, in turn, is enriched by the harmony between the medium and the new shape created.*

(c) The Mobile and the Stabile
Another interesting innovation is the mobile — a construction with the quality of actual movement. This seems a natural extension for the flower arranger inspired by the many rhythms of nature, whether the gusty tempo of a blowy day or the imperceptible breeze that ruffles the leaves and grasses. There is the movement of water, in a ripple or torrent, in falling leaves and drifting clouds. It is fun to create something with the new dimension of time, as motion in space — with movement as a dominant element. Alexander Calder was the innovator of kinetic compositions as a major art form and the delicate forms of his mobiles suspended in the air are inspirational.

Many items of our media lend well to a mobile. Plants that are light and delicate, that look well floating in space, like dried or skeletonised leaves, light seedheads and grasses, strips of bark and twigs, cones and nuts. These must be finely balanced and set so that there is complete freedom of movement. The correct physical balance enables each item to catch all the tiny, invisible air currents, so that there is constant motion. Mobility, lightness and a lyrical quality are the characteristics of an effective mobile. It should be soothing to watch, a poetry of motion. Fishing line is strong and almost invisible, so makes a suitable linkage between one item and the other. The true mobile moves on its own axis

FIG 50 — *A free-moving piece of driftwood forms the basis for this mobile. It sets in motion the separate units, which also rotate on their own axes, so that there is perpetual movement of each part and of the whole. Rings of wood make a pleasing frame for twisted pieces of seaweed trimmed with small skeletonised magnolia leaves to give an air of lightness and buoyancy (birds on the wing?). Each ring is placed at a different level to avoid a clash of movement, and adjusted so that one physically balances the other.*

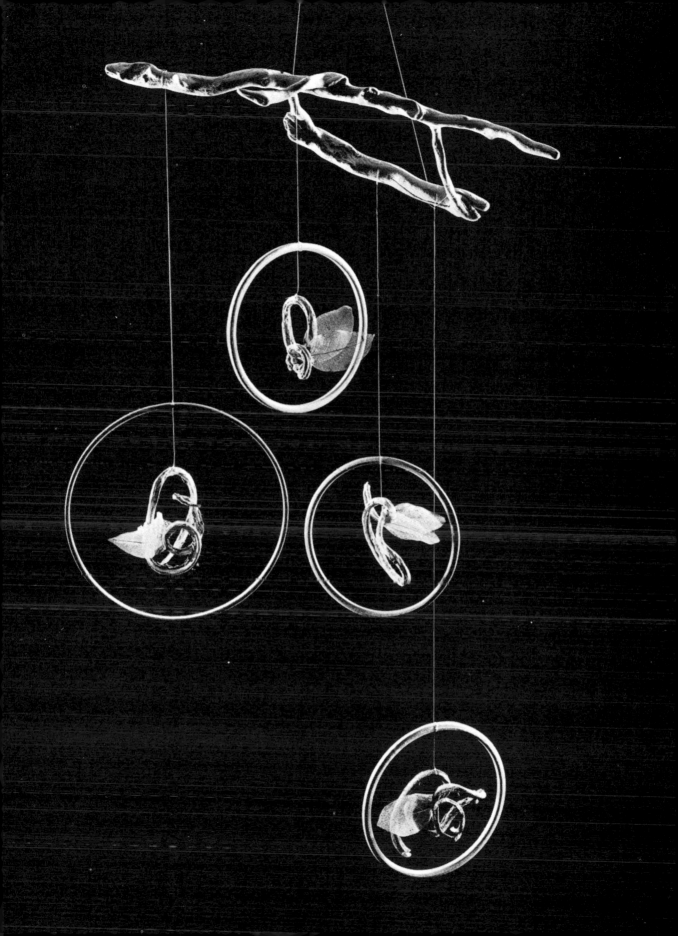

and also as part of the whole structure. To keep these free, the items must not touch or get entangled with each other so patience is called for in achieving this sensitive balance. An example is Fig. 50 which is made from tiny, skeletonised magnolia leaves and pieces of dried seaweed.

The stabile is ground anchored as opposed to the hanging aspect of the mobile. It has the quality of movement still, but this is illusionary not actual. It is movement of a different nature, that of soaring upwards. Again it is a challenge to play up to this illusion, to give the same buoyancy and liveliness as in the mobile.

A design of this kind must not look too firmly held to the ground, so the choice of container, base or method of anchorage is important. Space between the arrangement or the structure and container will strengthen the rhythm and add lightness. Materials with a strong movement can accentuate the rhythm. Wood, branches, grasses, seedhead, pointed flower spikes or round flowers arranged in a definite line. The aim is to strengthen the feeling of motion.

Constructions bearing aspects of the mobile and stabile are also interesting, like that in Fig. 51. Here the lower grouping — the stabile — is raised well out of the container and anchored on cane. The strong diagonal movement carries the eye upward to the mobile suspend-

ed in space, so that there is real and imagined movement complementing each other. The plant material here is fresh. Spheres of acid yellow bracts of *Euphorbia polychroma* glow like small suns, with reed stalks radiating all around. Small balls of wet oasis hold the moisture for the material; if the cut stems are singed the bracts last very well.

A similar combination can be seen in Colour Plate 9, this time with dried material. The top grouping is suspended from the picture frame, outlined by a 'moon' container, for another variation on the 'mobile' theme. The other group is lifted out of the container for illusionary movement. The two are connected with a swirl of blackened cane. The dyed grasses and tiny flowers (glixia) are colourful and 'burst' out in a scintillating sparkle of colour.

FIG 51 — *Movement implied and actual, created with a mobile and a stabile. It is interesting to note that in the picture the stabile looks more 'active' than the mobile! Such is the power of line to suggest and to create an illusion. Fact is not always stranger than fiction! The combination of the two rhythms is very pleasing, and this again would be a fascinating class title. It would literally get the whole show moving! Interest too would be focused on more than one level, which would be a great fillip to the overall presentation of the exhibits.*

9

CREATIVE TEACHING

A changing approach to the teaching of Flower Arrangement seems logical in the light of continuing progress. Many tutors now have a completely different approach which is more imaginative and creative.

In the past the pattern was largely set on imitative practices. The teacher would demonstrate a set pattern which the students copied. It was a straightforward but not very inspiring procedure and it tended to produce copies rather than original efforts. It also fostered the idea that there was only one way of designing — according to the book — which is stultifying, and guaranteed to put blinkers on the imagination.

The aim in creative teaching is to draw out the skills and talents of the students to make *their* participation the priority. It gets the arranger more fully involved in the learning process; she thinks for herself instead of accepting ready-made theories. In time she makes her own discoveries, her achievements give more personal satisfaction, and she gains independence and confidence. Natural flair is more likely to develop and to live this way, even if on a basis of greater trial and error.

Group discussion and assessment is often more instructional than a more one-sided teachers' criticism. In this way, the work can be considered more objectively so that the student can evaluate her own efforts more realistically. It is also a very stimulating way of working, as each student has the benefit of another's ideas and suggestions. Constructive criticism can lead to very interesting discussions and speculation on a wide variety of relevant topics.

A creative approach to designing will be based on the imaginative use of the medium of flower arranging. The student is encouraged to experiment, to study the plant material for its special qualities, and to use these in the most effective way rather than follow stereotyped patterns automatically. By experimenting and through observation new ways of designing may be discovered that are more stimulating and satisfying and which give more scope for originality.

This should engender a more flexible attitude for the student starts with an open mind and without too many pre-conceived, or set ideas of another person which can inhibit progress along individual lines.

The teacher can stimulate interest in other art forms to develop the appreciation of designing principles. Experiments with other media like clay or paint, could occasionally be introduced, or visits to art galleries and exhibitions to study the techniques and style of other artists. This would broaden outlook and make it easier to assess artistic work generally. It could be followed up by a discussion on the trends and emphasis of a particular era, notably that of the modern styles and their artistic intentions, and outlook. A good teacher will encourage her pupils to take the initiative at every opportunity but will still maintain control and guidance of the teaching procedure with its aim of progressive learning.

She sets the tone and pace by personal enthusiasm, knowledge and her own creative ability. It is a very responsible task. A creative teacher does more than just teach, she inspires and awakens the creative instincts of others.

Teaching the fundamentals of designing should be made as pleasurable as possible, to cultivate the right attitude towards the arranger's art. As this is in a perishable medium, the flower arranger must accept the impermanence of her efforts — much of the satisfaction and reward must come from creating the arrangement — from the actual experience of designing. All that is involved in the process, therefore, should be fulfilling and worthwhile.

10

SCHEDULES AND JUDGING

Changing attitudes, new designing methods and new concepts in using the medium of flower arrangement have demanded new conditions in competition and exhibition work. An abstract arrangement, for instance, is more or less a law unto itself, with its move away from the set pattern. It has become essential to make adjustments in the schedule and judging to suit the new approach.

We now see a gradual relaxing of restrictions to give the competitor greater freedom. The word 'Exhibit' is being used more and more, so the arranger can approach her theme in a less inhibited way. It allows more scope with style and presentation; placements and the general layout can be more original and individual. This also makes the judge's task a little easier and more enjoyable, since she can devote mind and energy to assessing artistic merit without the doubts and worries of ambiguous wording or restrictive statements. She can be more relaxed in evaluating form and content, and in getting attuned to each composition. It allows more time for concentration, often needed in assessing the more complex abstract statements.

Happily show committees and schedule makers generally have an increasingly more progressive approach, evident in schedule wording and class titles which encourage originality. Inspiring themes evoked by such classes as 'Space holds no Time', 'Art in Nature', 'In Perpetual Motion', 'Visual

Rhythm', 'A New Horizon', 'That the Future may Learn from the Past' — how could anyone be mundane with the challenge of such titles?

To encourage the most imaginative approach, the conforming conditions should be as flexible as possible. Dyed and painted items have been allowed in certain modern classes for some time. Now the 5th edition of NAFAS Schedule definitions says 'artificially coloured plant material may be used, unless otherwise stated in the Schedule'. In the past, this was strictly taboo and the trend was discouraged. Arrangers have proved that its discerning use can add design impact and often the right accent to an interpretation. In a theme like 'Black and White' or 'Psychedelic' the effect can be intensified with a little paint or dye. Often a slight touch of intense colour, from a fluorescent paint, will make all the difference to the colour rhythm. A colourful scheme can be made even more exciting with a blending of the hues involved in an item like wood or cane, or a strong colour contrast could be planned with a painted item to flatter the colour of the plant material. Base or container could be unified with an exact colour match in the arrangement.

Again, a perfect blending of accessory and material is sometimes difficult when the right plant is not available. A slight repetition of the right hue could be continued for extra rhythm and sparkle. One should avoid the crude and garish effects, and use the artificial effects discriminately and for a specific artistic purpose. We should soon weary of its over-use.

In an 'exhibit', the inclusion of non-floral material is permitted — this was allowed in the past only when the schedule permitted the use of accessories. Like the artificially coloured item, it gives added designing scope. Wire, plastic, glass and stone can all be incorporated into the design structure to become part of its rhythm or interest — perspex has a lightness and delicacy useful for mobiles; wire, in particular, has great adaptability and moulds easily to the particular line or effect required. I have used orange electric power cable in the cover picture, to give a smooth, rhythmical sequence which leads up to the strelitzia flowers. Plant material here has the right complementary interest in its bold sculptural qualities. The design pattern integrates the two disparate objects into a unified composition, so that both work for the ultimate design effect — which should be the criterion for the use of foreign materials.

To be sympathetic, the judge must be equally attuned to progress. Evaluation of new art forms can no longer be on traditional standards only. Every effort should be made to appreciate the intent of the designer in an abstract or unconventional design, where assessment will not necessarily follow the conventional judging pattern. The new is sometimes startling, and the judge needs time for adjustment. Personally, I find judging the more progressive classes easier when they are not too specifically categorised. A division of styles is convenient and practical between old and new, but the true artistic temperament works more often than not on the moment's inspiration, without the thought of definite categories or a prescribed style. By the same token, the judge can respond more intuitively to each exhibit as a creative whole when there is not the distraction of too much analysis.

One's intuitive senses can be bogged down with the worry of whether it is in this or that style, abstract or not so abstract. It is a much better practice to try and feel the whole, to search for meaning in its form, before the critical evaluation.

It should then become easier to assess and to judge on the merit of each exhibit which, in the end, is the deciding factor in any style.

The same principles are involved in all designs; it is merely the presentation that varies. The 'free', the unconventional, those that break away from the traditional, must be assessed in relation to the change of form and concept, but as their visual appeal and artistry is still determined by the same universal factors, the same criterion applies to their judging.

FIG 52 – *The fewer the restrictions imposed on the competitor, the more freedom is permitted in placements, style and choice of materials. Apart from details of the dimensions of the space allowed per competitor, curbing conditions should be kept to a minimum, and a great deal of bother and speculation is saved if the word 'Exhibit' is used, or better still just the class title by itself. The composition here would need as unrestrictive a schedule wording as possible to justify the unconventional staging.*

FIG 53 — *A free standing background made of chipboard painted white gives scope to incorporate background interest with that of the arrangement. Twigs painted black, to stress their beautiful linear quality, portray 'Calligraphy'. The circular forms fixed to the background carry the eye through a progression of similar shapes from the base and front of the arrangement to the rear. The contrast and repetition of black and white dramatises and gives wonderful clarity to the design, and strengthens the interpretation.*

11

EXPERIMENTS WITH STAGING

The flower show or an exhibition is a grand opportunity for displaying new trends and activities. To meet the challenge of the ever developing innovations, new and better ways of presenting the exhibits are continually being tried out by progressive clubs.

Much has been done to improve staging generally. Mercifully the days of complete dedication to the corrugated niche — useful in its day, but no longer considered satisfactory or effective for every presentation — are over. The aim now is to design backgrounds appropriate to a given theme or title. This avoids the monotony of uniform backgrounds, and gives the overall display more style and variety. At the 1971 NAFAS Festival in London, entitled 'Serendipity', the exhibitor was greatly helped in such classes as 'Peak of Great Serenity', 'Shibui' and 'Charivari', with background colours that were truly inspiring for the themes involved, and which strongly accented and enhanced the exhibits.

The exhibitor herself often takes the initiative of designing her own background, which can be planned as part of the composition. It is then considered in the light of a design unit and not merely an area to define the proportions of the arrangement. In the past, the arranger concerned herself mainly in terms of height, width and depth of the niche provided; now the background is valued for its contribution to the line, form, colour, texture and character of the arrangement. The background exerts its own design force and so is chosen with as much care as the rest of the compositional units. Its colour and texture can give added definition to that of the arrangement. This is especially important in the design where large areas of space play an active part — the advancing or receding nature of the back-cloth will exert different influences on the spatial element, the rhythm and force of the design.

There are so many exciting possibilities with cloth and paints for a whole range of effects. Hessian, felt, suede, velvet, brushed nylon etc., have distinctive surface qualities and a whole range of marvellous colours, so that even when very little is used colour and texture contrasts can have a real punch.

Colour appeal can be really exploited — mustard yellows against navy blue or a deep maroon red — lilac and cerise or magenta with lime green, pale orange and pale pink. Or it can be achieved with paints, which are cheaper and more easily changed. Spray paints make for quick and smooth finishes; powder paints can be washed off and are easily mixed for subtle effects — several different hues can be blended more or less haphazardly for a varied colour effect with greater depth.

Texture effects can be varied in the same way, with a

Study the two arrangements overleaf.

FIG 54 — This abstract arrangement and that facing it have the same theme; the same accessory, base and container is used in each. It is the way in which they are staged that differs. It is interesting to compare the varying effects. In the first example the diagonal line inspired by the accessory continued by cane shapes and a radiating line of reedmace. Dried gourds give balance and a contrast of shape. The back-cloth creates an uninterrupted and pleasantly textured surface against which to view the arrangement.

FIG 55 — This is another way of presenting the theme of the previous composition, now seen against a white free-standing background. This is totally involved, through its motif, which echoes the shape of the accessory, with the line of the arrangement, and so functions more obviously as part of the design. Line is more decisively contained in one direction than in the other design, where the cane creates a more varied series of movements. In this second grouping, the gourds are painted white, the reedmace black, to sharpen their contours and give a stronger colour contrast. Both presentations are interesting in different ways.

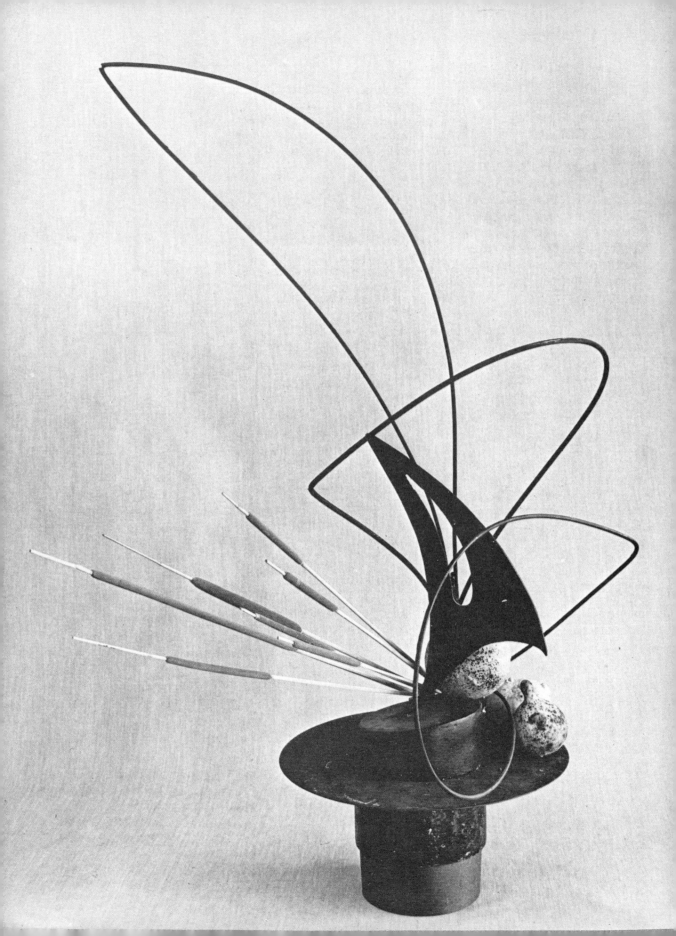

blending of rough and smooth areas to create shadows and a more animated surface. Ordinary chipboard, or the reverse side of hardboard, has a very interesting texture, which is not too distracting as a background. For in all these projects the effect must not be overdone. Too much background activity will detract from the arrangement in the foreground. It is only when one works for the other in a totally integrated sequence that the presentation is visually satisfying.

The background can also promote the line and form of the arrangement, by drawing the eye to certain areas, creating added rhythm and depth. A shape, motif or stem of plant material can be fixed to the background itself. It must of course fall in with the contour and movement of the composition, not as an extra decoration. This again has interesting possibilities.

Lighting is another device for enhancing an exhibit. It can accent, subdue or create the desired atmosphere. There has long been an awareness of light as an essential part of the visual arts, with its value as a medium exploited. Its use has reached a high level of sophistication in many modern art exhibitions, with electrically controlled devices and light constructions. Experiments are also under way at the flower show, though to date its full use has yet to be employed, obviously because so much more is involved in its effective staging and in the resources available.

The way light is directed on to the composition must be thoroughly planned, as it will greatly affect the character and much will depend on the effect required; adjustable lights can be swivelled until the right areas are involved. Sometimes shadows are the main objective, which are created as a major part of the design — and very effective these can be. A background enlivened with diffused light can increase the emotional impact, or a play of coloured lights can be used for a gay exciting effect. Wouldn't it be marvellous if every niche was fitted with a lighting device that could be adjusted with coloured filters, so that one could select the hue, or mixture of hues, to suit the mood and quality of each arrangement? One would be using light as colour in a really positive way.

Again, in a display of abstract arrangements, colour of background or of the composition could be distorted with the use of near ultra-violet radiant energy called 'black light'. Items painted with luminous and fluorescent paints would glow magnificently, especially in a darkened setting. Further exciting effects could be achieved with spotlights at floor and ceiling level. Coloured lights on all-white exhibits would add a touch of magic, and moving lights another dimension. These techniques offer great possibilities and scope for future innovations.

12

CHANGE
AND CHALLENGE

Abstract arrangements with their non-realistic qualities and constructions of plant material in altered forms, some of the very stark modern designs, are in great contrast to the traditional and naturalistic styles.

Those dedicated to the old, find it hard to accept the departure from convention, in the same way that in the other arts, some resent the by-passing of the traditional sculpture, based on classical form or the realistic, re-presentational painting.

An artist, in any sphere, is affected by the social, cultural and general conditions of the times he lives in — this is reflected in the form of the artistic expression.

In an age where the way of life and our understanding of the world is changing rapidly, it is difficult for any project to stand still for long. The present is a time of astounding scientific discoveries, fast communication, the age of the machine, speed, landing on the moon, and exploring the unknown. So it is not surprising that our arts are changing as much as our knowledge of the world.

Now that flower arranging is becoming recognised as an art form, it is inevitable it should be influenced too; that flower arrangers should also respond to world-wide artistic trends, moving with and adapting to the times. I think it is very exciting and wonderful to be part of the making of its history.

Greater knowledge of design and understanding of

the aims of designing spurs the arranger to greater activity so new techniques continually emerge. Each discovery is the stimulation to the next.

Growth means change. This we must accept if flower arranging is to remain an art. Its freshness and vigour cannot be maintained with apathy. To quote Sir Herbert Read, 'Change is the condition of Art remaining Art'.

The new is criticised — that is inevitable too. All changes are not always good changes, and what suits one medium may not adapt as well to another. That is part of experimenting, without which one would never know anything. The extreme in any art form is never the most popular. This does not mean it is no good. It often takes time for the eye and mind to get adjusted; so the new is often not appreciated until long afterwards — sadly for the artist concerned.

The chief concern perhaps of those who love their flowers, is the lack or absence of flowers in very modern designs. There has been much speculation and controversy over major awards at National or area shows when these have included the very minimum of flowers, or none at all, and especially when evaluated against those with a profusion of beautiful blooms.

Perhaps the system should be changed, especially in competition. Maybe a certain accepted division is called for, one for arrangements where the accent is more on flowers and plant material generally, used in the traditional way, and the other for those which are pure design, which could include 'arrangement' in a wider form, where design is the subject rather than merely the means of putting plant material together.

This would give the best of both worlds. Those primarily interested in growing and displaying flowers as flowers would have the assurance that traditional and conventional arranging is to continue. The firm traditionalists prefer to continue along well trodden, conventional paths, and are happier with the known and the time-tested. Many too, like to progress without being too extreme or avant-garde, preferring moderation in new ventures and keeping one finger on convention as it were.

With this new system they need not force their pace of progress, and could let things evolve with time or inclination. At the same time it would give the arranger who sees plant material as an art medium and considers it in terms of artistic possibilities, every chance to develop and to enlarge its designing possibilities. The enthusiast needs the stimulation of new outlets and fresh challenges, with freedom to develop ideas. It would be a pity to curb the enthusiasm.

Is there any reason why we cannot have it both ways? Is it not possible for all styles to be tolerated even if not universally practised? Why not enjoy,

or at least consider, each differing approach in the light of its special contribution to the flower arrangement movement as a whole? One could then appreciate natural beauty and accept the wider contribution of flower arranging as an art form.

FIG 56 — *Flowers as flowers in a naturalistic design. A classical timeless style, idealising the beauty of the material. The flowers are arranged to resemble as closely as possible their appearance when growing naturally. The arrangement is simple and easy to live with.*

FIG 57 — *The plant material here is considered as nothing more than a number of design units. The major interest lies in the intriguing line of the alliums and the pattern, interesting and varied throughout the design, which they create.*

FIG 58 — *There is the same design form here as in the previous arrangement, with added textural and colour interest conferred by the purple allium flowers. These give the arrangement a greater variety of contrasting elements, but the spatial and linear interest is not as forceful as in the previous example.*

FIG 59 — 'The Power and the Glory' — *The material here is used expressively for an arrangement with an emotional and evocative quality. The theme is communicated by the dominant characteristics of line, form, texture and colour in the wood and the flowers.*

FIG 60 — *An abstract design with items which lend themselves to a series of emphasis points with strong form and textural interest. Here the alliums are at the seedhead stage. It shows how interesting and useful they are at many different stages of their growth.*

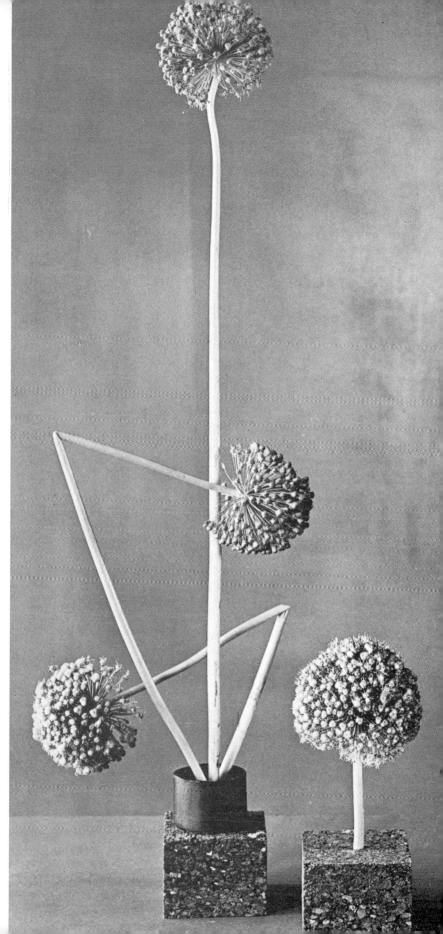

FIG 61 — *Yet another variety of allium, one with a lighter, less compact form. The radiating pattern ending in dainty flowers is quite scintillating and this looks best prominently displayed in solo style. An exciting relationship of line and space is set up with twisted loops of cane and an interesting container.*

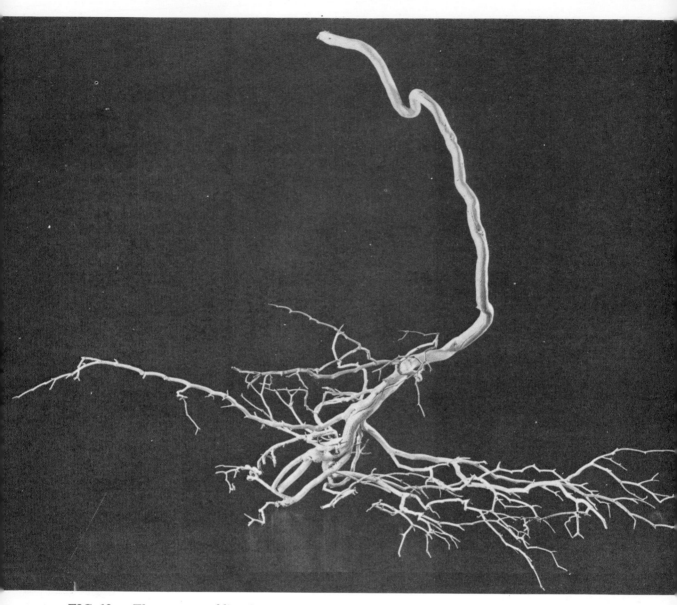

FIG 62 — *The poetry of line in
a branch painted white and
turned upside down.*

FIG 63 — Straight lines and Curves. *Such things, and the surfaces of solid forms produced out of these by laths and rulers and squares', Plato, long ago said 'are always beautiful, with a beauty that is natural and absolute, in no way dependent on other things or the senses'.*